WOK
Cookbook

Chinese, Japanese, Thai and Korean recipes

Best Traditional Asian Recipes

Livia McDaniel

TABLE OF CONTENT

Introduction to the wok

The wok is a pot originating from China with a conical shape and a rounded or hemispherical bottom.

Therefore, a symbol of Chinese cuisine, the wok is the same age as the Great Wall: 2000 years ago, it was born in the Asian countryside. Initially widespread and used in poor environments, such as the eastern countryside, it was used to cook more than one food in the same pan to save both on the tool and on fuel. Today it has lost its character linked to the cheapness of the product and has spread all over the world and in restaurants and is not disdained even by great chefs.

The wok, despite the various evolutions, has always maintained a fundamental characteristic, that of weight. It is in fact the heaviness of the wok that allows it to maintain heat for a long time.

The flared shape with the very small terminal point in direct contact with the flame is not only a quirk but has its own function: it allows you to fry immersed and in a very short time even using a little oil.

The short cooking over a low flame allows you to quickly cook vegetables, meat and fish, leaving the flavors and nutritional properties intact.

This also applies if we are talking about different types of cooking: the wok is also ideal for stewing, braising, slow cooking, boiling, browning, smoking and even steaming. In any case, the advantage is the speed of cooking without adding fat, translated: as lighter and healthier cooking.

Chapter 1:
Characteristics of the Wok & How to Choose the Most Suitable for your Needs

The wok differs from normal pans due to its hemispherical shape, higher and rounded walls and a diameter that varies from 30 to 80 cm. The bottom can be concave or flat: the latter makes the wok more comfortable because it can be adapted to all hobs.

The original version of the wok provided the presence of two metal handles, which today have been covered with wood.
Another very common variant is the one with a single long handle, which, unlike the classic version, makes it less manageable.
Especially for beginners, the model with a double handle is recommended: the wok, being forged in steel, iron or cast iron, is quite heavy and for those who are not very familiar with this pan it is better to start cooking with the classic model.

The new models are also available with different materials than cast iron, in fact, you can also find woks in aluminum and even coated with Teflon, a highly non-stick material, or with a Pyrex glass lid. The glass lid allows you to keep cooked foods warm and cook quickly without having to remove the lid continuously.

The wok allows food to be cooked evenly as the heat is distributed evenly along the sides of the pan. You can cook a greater quantity of foods at the same time, and you will have the advantage that they flavor each other.
It is also suitable for healthy and dietetic cooking because it is a pan in all respects, and you can cook without oil and without adding fat.

HOW TO USE THE WOK

The wok is mainly used for cooking fast foods. But you can also cook something else. Thanks to its shape and size, the wok can also be used for steam cooking. Some models are sold with grids that are used to arrange the food, while the water for cooking is placed underneath.

It is also excellent for cooking fish, especially if flavored or stewed, as the pan lends itself very well to make the food taste better. Being non-stick, nothing sticks, and cooking is homogeneous at every point.

It is more convenient to fry because, its narrower shape below and wider at the top, allow you to fry with less oil. If you use the same grill for steam cooking, you can drain freshly fried foods while keeping them warm.

WHICH OILS TO USE FOR WOK COOKING?

With wok cooking, it's not just the flavor of the oil you have to think about, but also the smoke point.

When you cook in a wok, you're usually preparing a quick meal at a very high temperature. This means that the best wok oil will have a high smoke point and a flavor that is neutral or complementary to the type of dish you're cooking.

The best oils for a wok are coconut oil, toasted sesame oil, soybean oil, canola oil, avocado oil, and peanut and grape seed oil.

Chapter 2:
Characteristics & Differences between Chinese, Thai Japanese, & Korean Cuisine

In this chapter, we will see what the main characteristics of the four best known Asian cuisines in the world are.

BASIC FEATURES OF CHINESE CUISINE

Chinese cuisine is one of the best known and most widespread cuisines in the world. Below we will see what are the basic ingredients that are used in this type of cuisine.

- **Sauces.**

The basis of Chinese cuisine is sauces. Present in almost all Chinese dishes, the most commonly used sauces are four: light soy sauce, dark soy sauce, oyster sauce and hoisin sauce. Light soy sauce, less dense and saltier, is mainly used to marinate foods, especially meat and fish, while dark soy sauce, denser and less salty, is used for cooking braised meats and stews. Oyster sauce, on the other hand, is obtained by boiling oysters with sugar and soy sauce. Thick and tasty, it is used in meat and vegetable recipes, both as an accompanying sauce in which to dip the food, and in cooking to fry the ingredients. Hoisin sauce is a sauce with a salty and strong taste, with a dark color and is obtained from fermented soybeans, garlic, vinegar, chili pepper and sugar. It is generally used to glaze meat and to marinate dishes, especially when they are intended to be cooked on the grill.

- **Oil.**

Another key element of Chinese cuisine is oil. The oils used are always seed oils, usually the most used is peanut oil, while if you prefer a more delicate flavor, it is better to opt for soybean, corn or sunflower oil.

- **Rice wine.**

In addition to the well-known sauces and different types of oil, there are other liquid seasonings that are often found in Chinese recipes. One of these is rice wine, an alcoholic beverage that derives from the fermentation of must obtain from rice processing. Typically, it is used to flavor a variety of foods, sauces, and pickles.

- **Spices.**

Spices play a very important role in Chinese dishes. Among the most present is ginger, used fresh or in powder. For the spicier dishes, Sichuan pepper is used, with a spicy and strong flavor, giving the dishes a strong and intense aroma. On the other hand, the five-spice powder is irreplaceable, a particular blend made with Sichuan pepper, star anise, cloves, cinnamon and fennel seeds.

- **Mushrooms.**

If mushrooms are among the ingredients of the recipe you want to make, it is important to get Chinese mushrooms that can be found dried in specialized shops. Two are the most common: Tonku mushrooms, also known by the Japanese name of Shiitake, and Mu'er mushrooms, black mushrooms also known as "Judas' ears", characterized by a delicate flavor and crunchy texture.

- **Bamboo and bean sprouts.**

Another category of ingredients peculiar to Chinese cuisine, which cannot be replaced with alternatives from Western cuisine, are bamboo shoots and bean sprouts. Bamboo shoots, very popular in China, can be purchased canned, both whole and pre-sliced. Before using them, they should be rinsed with cold water and left to soak for about fifteen minutes. Bean sprouts are also found canned, but it is possible to find them fresh too. And the latter is undoubtedly the best solution. To recognize its freshness, it is sufficient to observe the stem: if it is white it means that the buds are fresh, if it is yellowish or brown it is better not to buy them.

- **Vegetables.**

The dishes of Chinese cuisine, even when they are based on meat or fish, are rich in vegetables. Many are vegetables that also characterize Mediterranean cuisines, such as aubergines, peppers and carrots, others are typical of China. Among these are Chinese cabbage, of which there are several varieties, and water chestnuts.

- **Rice.**

When one thinks of Chinese cuisine, rice is one of the first courses that come to mind. Served white, to accompany meat, fish and vegetable courses, or enriched with other ingredients, rice is among the dishes most present on Chinese tables and can be declined in numerous variations. The important thing, however, is to use the right variety. The most suitable rice is long grain rice.

- **Noodles.**

Another important element of Chinese cuisine is noodles. There are numerous types, which differ from each other in length, width, thickness and construction ingredients. Among the most common are noodles prepared with wheat flour, mainly soft, rice noodles and soy noodles, which are bought dry.

BASIC FEATURES OF JAPANESE CUISINE

The ingredients of Japanese cuisine are quite different from Western ones. The sweet, sour and salty flavors characterize this particularly delicate gastronomy with subtle and balanced aromas.

- **Soy Sauce**.

The basis of Japanese cuisine is soy sauce. Soy sauce made from fermented soybeans and wheat. Used in many Japanese recipes to add flavor. There are mainly 5 varieties. Koikuchi: Typical of the Kanto area produced with half soy and half wheat. Usukuchi: typical of Kansai, it is slightly saltier than the previous one but lighter in color due to the use of a rice fermentation liquid (Amazake). Tamari: typical of the Chubu area, it is produced with a lot of soy and little wheat, therefore it is darker and stronger in flavor. Shyro: unlike Tamari, it has a lot of wheat and little soy, making it clearer and less savory. Saishikomi: Obtained from a double fermentation which makes it dark and with a very intense flavor.

- **Mirin.**

Another basic element of Japanese cuisine is mirin. Mirin is a transparent sweet liquid with very low alcohol content (it is also known as sweet sake), and it is the ingredient that constitutes the sweet component of Japanese dishes, giving the sauces an unmistakable sweetness and silkiness.

- **Sake.**

Sake is the third staple of Japanese cuisine. By now we practically all know sake, the famous "rice wine", and it is also one of the simplest ingredients to find. What perhaps not everyone knows is that in addition to being a much-loved drink, it is also often used for the preparation of sauces and for marinating ingredients, and represents, together with mirin and soy sauce, the essential triad for the preparation of sauces and condiments.

- **Katsuobushi.**

Katsuobushi consists of dried flakes of bonito tuna and represents the basis of dashi broth, fundamental in Japanese cuisines like soy sauce and mirin, to flavor dishes and for basic preparations. Katsuobushi is also often used as a garnish to flavor dishes, but its main use is to prepare dashi broth.

- **Rice.**

Rice is another of the fundamental elements of Japanese cuisine. There are several varieties, which you can find quite easily even in online stores or ethnic cuisine shops.

- **Algae.**

Nori seaweed is probably the most widespread and well-known, we are used to seeing it, in fact, in hosomaki and onigiri. It is found on the market quite easily, you can find it in sheets, thin and crunchy, and you can use it both to wrap rice, as in the examples mentioned above, or you can break it up to sprinkle it on the dishes. Since nori seaweed absorbs liquids quite quickly, it is always better to use it at the last moment to wrap the dishes and keep them crunchy for longer. Kombu seaweed forms, together with katsuobushi, the basis for preparing dashi broth. It is an ingredient that cannot be missing, and which can also be used to flavor the rice cooking water. Before using it, always remember to rinse it under cold water to remove the layer of salt.

- **Miso**

is one of the fundamental ingredients of Japanese cuisine and is a paste obtained from fermented soybeans to which rice or barley is added and is an extremely versatile ingredient that can be used in soups, sauces or marinades. It is mainly produced with soy, salt and koji, but there are numerous variations, each with its own flavor and distinctive characteristics. Based on the composition and degree of fermentation, it is classified according to 3 colors: Shiro miso, white miso, has the most delicate flavor, dark miso, santoku-miso, up to red miso, aka miso, with a stronger flavor (and longer fermentation).

- **Noodles.**

In addition to rice, another fundamental component for Japanese recipes is noodles, which can be eaten hot or cold, in broth or sautéed on the plate. The most commonly used noodles are definitely soba (buckwheat noodles) and udon (soft wheat flour noodles).

- **Wasabi & Ginger.**

Wasabi and ginger are two other essential elements of Japanese cuisine, which you will find present in many recipes. Wasabi is a spicy green sauce made from the root of the plant of the same name (Japanese horseradish), which grows mainly near the waterways of the Izu Peninsula. Wasabi is usually used in sushi, it is placed between the slice of raw fish and the rice, and you can find it in a tube, or in powder.

In Japanese cuisine, fresh ginger is also used a lot, it is usually grated in various sauces or condiments, even if its best-known use is as tsukemono: ginger (gari) is cut into thin slices and marinated in a solution of water, sugar and vinegar.

BASIC FEATURES OF KOREAN CUISINE

Korean cuisine is the result of a very ancient tradition, with origins from prehistoric times. It is mainly made up of rice, meat and vegetable dishes and differs from other oriental culinary traditions in a large number of side dishes available for each meal.

- **Rice.**

Rice is one of the essential foods of Korean cuisine. The variety used most is like that used in Japan. The variety is the short-grain variety and Koreans eat it almost every day. A rice cooker is usually used to steam it, although it can be easily prepared using a pot with a lid. Steamed rice can also be cooked with other grains such as barley or wheat.

- **Soy Sauce.**

Soy sauce is one of the most important condiments in Korean cuisine, and some Asian cuisines in general. In Korea, there are three types of soy sauce that differ in taste, texture, amount of salt and in the dishes in which they are used. These three types of soy sauce are jinganjang (dark color and strong aroma), junganjang (brown color with a milder aroma) and mulgun ganjang (light color and very mild taste).

- **Sesame Oil.**

Sesame oil, this oil is a staple ingredient in Korean cuisine. It is used for preparing various types of food such as soups, porridges and sauces.

- **Perilla Leaves & Seeds.**

The perilla herb belongs to the mint family and its leaves have a strong flavor, with notes of licorice. The leaves can be eaten fresh in salads, used as a wrapper for rolling meat or rice, or the leaves can be shredded and used as a condiment. Perilla leaves can also be prepared in other ways: for example, stir-fried with other vegetables.

- **Fish Sauce.**

This sauce is used in the most famous Korean dish, kimchi, and has a very strong anchovy flavor and is particularly salty. Fish sauce is also used in the preparation of stews and soups.

- **Chili Paste.**

Although hot peppers were recently introduced to South Korea, they have become a key ingredient in Korean cuisine. Chili paste is a condiment made from fermented red chili peppers with glutinous rice, fermented soybeans, and salt. This paste is used in many dishes such as bibimbap and tteokbokki, in salads or in stews.

- **Chili Powder.**

This powder is used in many dishes and there is both a spicy type and a less spicy and sweeter type. The spicy version of this powder is used to prepare Kimchi for example.

BASIC FEATURES OF THAI CUISINE

Thai cuisine stands out among Asian and oriental cuisines in general for the balance of the five fundamental flavors: sweet, sour, salty, bitter and umami. Herbs, spices and rice are the basic ingredients of almost all typical recipes in Thailand, in addition to fish and meat.

- **Fish Sauce.**

It's the secret to almost all Thai dishes. It is obtained by fermenting fish, usually anchovies, for a long time covered with salt. It has a terrible smell but only those who cook smell it. Once mixed with the other ingredients, in fact, whoever eats the dish does not notice it at all.

- **Oyster Sauce.**

This is another sauce widely used in Thai cuisine that is thick, dark, and has both a sweet and salty flavor.

- **Lemongrass**

is one of the basic elements of curry paste and is widely used in oriental cuisine both in soups and cut into salads. The slightly rounded base deprived of the external part which is very hard is mainly used. The tenderest part is thinly sliced or pounded in a mortar to release the oil. Often, being quite hard, it is put whole in soups and then removed after cooking. Its smell is very volatile, so it needs to be fresh or frozen. It is useless to buy the dry one because it absolutely does not maintain the aroma of fresh lemongrass. It has a pungent taste and a citrus smell, without having acidity.

- **Tamarind.**

The unripe fruit is very sour and is used for various dishes, the sweeter ripe fruit is used for desserts. Both the pulp and the juice are used.

- **Galangal:**

The rhizomes of Galangal are used in various traditional Thai cuisines from curries to soups to salads, the best example being Tom Kha Gai. Galangal is not typically eaten as a main dish but is used to add aroma and flavor to dishes. The root of the plant is related to ginger, which is why they look alike, but their flavors are very distinct from each other; thus, one should not confuse them because one cannot be used to replace the other.

- **Kaffir Lime Leaves.**

One of the most popular and widely used ingredients in Thai cooking, from curries, salads, soups, and stir-fries. Thais also use kaffir lime leaves with steamed seafood to reduce the fishy smell and enhance the citrus aroma. Although the leaves are edible, most Thais only consume them when they have been thinly sliced for dishes like Choo Chee and Panang curry or Tod Mun Pla.

Most pasta shares the same recipe using fresh herbs and spices such as cumin, chilies, galangal, lemongrass, red shallots and garlic. Other ingredients such as kaffir lime vine or zest, coriander roots or prawn paste can be added to make the paste different. In Thailand, pastes are traditionally made by pounding and mixing many herbs and spices together with a pestle and mortar.

Ready-made Thai curry paste is a time- and life-saving product, especially for beginners. Thai curry pastes typically come in three colors: red, green, and yellow. These colors are not simply aesthetic, they usually tell us the flavor of these pastes. The red curry paste is bright and heavily spiced with dried red chilies. Green curry paste is believed to be the fizziest curry paste of all since it is created using vivid green Bird's Eye chili peppers.

The least spicy of the three, yellow curry paste gets its color from turmeric and Indian-style yellow curry powder.

Chapter 3:
Fast Tips & Tricks

Before cooking with the wok, some preliminary operations are necessary. In fact, it is necessary to proceed with a series of boiling with water and bicarbonate to eliminate any chemical residue. Then, you can move on to the various types of cooking, taking care to prepare all the ingredients to be cooked.

- When steaming with a wok, don't forget the steamer basket. The wok can also be used with a grill resting on the top of the pot. All the fats will fall into the lower part of the wok and allow you to cook light and tasty dishes.

- Induction hobs should be avoided if you want to cook food quickly and evenly. Gas hobs allow you to control the flame's intensity.

- If you use a wok for sautéing, be cautious to heat the oil first and then add your ingredients; if you don't, your food will lose its crunch.

- The idea that the wok should always be utilized hot is one that can be applied to any preparation. Therefore, the pot must be cooked over the fire by gradually adding the various items.

- When adding additional ingredients to the wok to be cooked concurrently, keep in mind to stir them transversally rather than in a circular motion to help them cling as much as possible to the extremely hot pan's sides.

- Always use a wooden or silicone ladle to stir the ingredients; this will prevent scratching the pan's non-stick coating.

- You can quickly stew your food or thicken the sauces you are making by combining the cover with the wok.

- How to clean a wok. Just put hot water inside the original wok if it doesn't have a non-stick coating. After giving it some time to rest, drain it and give it a gentle cleaning with a soft cloth or sponge. To prevent rust, you can occasionally polish it with cooking oil. On the other hand, the Teflon-coated wok may be cleaned with hot water and some dishwashing solutions.

Chapter 4:
Recipes

Almond Chicken

Chinese Recipes

Preapering	Servings	Cooking	Calories
15 Minutes	2 People	20 Minutes	348

Ingredients:

- 8.8 oz of chicken breast
- 2.1 oz of peeled almonds
- 2 tbsp of soy sauce
- 2 spring onions
- 1 tsp of freshly grated ginger
- 1 and ½ tbsp vegetable oil
- Rice flour to taste

Nutritional Values:

Carb:	12 Gr.
Sugars:	5 Gr.
Proteins:	27 Gr.
Fats:	6 Gr.
Sodium:	530 Mg.

Steps for Cooking:

1. Almonds should first be lightly toasted for two minutes in a nonstick pan. To prevent burning the almonds, turn them off frequently.

2. The chicken should now be chopped into roughly equal-sized cubes.

3. Chicken cubes should be placed in a bowl, then rice flour should be added and combined with a wooden spoon.

4. The spring onions should be washed, sliced, and added to the wok along with the ginger and seed oil.

5. After a brief period of cooking, add the chicken. Stirring often, simmer for 10 minutes.

6. Add the soy sauce and two tablespoons of boiling water after ten minutes. Add the almonds after you've blended. If required, season with salt and pepper, stir constantly, and simmer for a further 3 minutes.

7. Now that the chicken and almonds are prepared, divide it into two bowls and serve.

Almond Tofu

Chinese Recipes

Preapering	Servings	Cooking	Calories
15 Minutes	2 People	10 Minutes	160

Ingredients:

- 8 tbsp soy sauce
- 1 tbsp of seed oil
- 1 pinch of garlic powder
- ½ tsp chopped fresh ginger
- ½ tsp of onion powder
- 14 oz of tofu
- 1 tbsp of olive oil
- 1 small red pepper
- 3 small onions
- ½ cup of chopped celery
- 1 cup of cold water
- 1 tbsp of cornstarch
- 4 tbsp of toasted almonds

Nutritional Values:

Carb:	3 Gr.
Sugars:	2 Gr.
Proteins:	14 Gr.
Fats:	10 Gr.
Sodium:	110 Mg.

Steps for Cooking:

1. Put 4 tbsp of soy sauce, olive oil, garlic powder, ginger and onion powder in a bowl and mix well.

2. Cut the tofu into cubes, put it in the bowl with the marinade and mix well. Leave to marinate for 2 hours, stirring occasionally.

3. Wash the pepper, remove the seeds and cut it into strips.

4. Remove the green part from the onions, wash them and cut them into rings.

5. Heat the seed oil in the wok and then sauté the onions, pepper and celery and two tbsp of water, and cook, covered, for 10 minutes.

6. Put in the cup with the rest of the water, the rest of the soy sauce and the cornstarch and mix well.

7. Add the cornstarch to the vegetables, stir and cook until the sauce has completely thickened.

8. Remove the vegetables and sauce from the wok and add the tofu, marinade and toasted almonds to the wok.

9. Mix well and cook for 5 minutes, stirring often. Divide the vegetables and sauce between two plates, add the tofu and toasted almonds and serve.

Cantonese Rice

Chinese Recipes

Preapering	Servings	Cooking	Calories
20 Minutes	2 People	30 Minutes	225

Ingredients:

- 5.2 oz of basmati rice
- 1.7 oz of cooked ham
- 1 egg
- 2.6 oz of blanched peas
- 1 tbsp of soy sauce
- 2 tbsp of sesame seed oil
- 2 tsp of peanut oil
- Salt to taste

Nutritional Values:

Carb:	29 Gr.
Sugars:	3 Gr.
Proteins:	9 Gr.
Fats:	9 Gr.
Sodium:	139 Mg.

Steps for Cooking:

1. Rice should be thoroughly rinsed until the water is clear.

2. Place the rice in a pot, add ice water to cover, and cook until the water has entirely been absorbed.

3. After cooking, place it on a plate to cool completely and set it aside.

4. In a dish, crack the egg, sprinkle some salt over it, and beat it with a fork.

5. Pour the egg into the wok after heating the peanut oil. Cook for a few minutes while stirring frequently.

6. Cook for 2 minutes after adding the ham and peas.

7. Add the rice, sesame oil, and soy sauce at this point.

8. Turn off the mixer after thoroughly incorporating all of the ingredients.

9. Serve the Cantonese rice in two bowls, divided.

Chicken with Lemon

Chinese Recipes

Preapering	Servings	Cooking	Calories
25 Minutes	2 People	10 Minutes	321

Ingredients:

- 10.5 oz of chicken breast
- Flour to taste
- Salt and pepper to taste
- ½ lemon
- ½ glass of water
- 2 tsp of cornstarch
- 1 tsp of brown sugar
- 1 tsp of soy sauce
- Peanut oil to taste

Nutritional Values:

Carb:	6 Gr.
Sugars:	2 Gr.
Proteins:	40 Gr.
Fats:	6 Gr.
Sodium:	250 Mg.

Steps for Cooking:

1. Wash the lemon, grate the zest and squeeze the juice into a bowl.

2. Wash the chicken, cut it first in half and then into cubes.

3. Place the chicken in a bowl and add salt, pepper and flour. Stir and coat the chicken pieces completely in the flour.

4. Heat the seed oil in the wok and, when it's hot, put the chicken to brown on all sides.

5. When the chicken is well browned, remove it from the wok and set aside.

6. Put the lemon juice, water, cornstarch, sugar and soy sauce in the wok.

7. Mix well, let it thicken for 1 minute and then put the chicken back in.

8. Cook for 4 minutes, then add the lemon zest and mix well.

9. At this point, switch off, divide the chicken and lemon sauce between two plates and serve.

Chicken with Mushrooms

Chinese Recipes

Preapering	Servings	Cooking	Calories
20 Minutes	2 People	20 Minutes	360

Ingredients:

- 7 oz of chicken breast
- 5.2 oz of shitake mushrooms
- 5.2 oz of bamboo in a jar
- 2 tsp of potato starch
- 1 clove of minced garlic
- Soy sauce to taste
- Seed oil to taste
- Salt and pepper to taste

Nutritional Values:

Carb:	3 Gr.
Sugars:	1 Gr.
Proteins:	34 Gr.
Fats:	6 Gr.
Sodium:	270 Mg.

Steps for Cooking:

1. Clean the mushrooms well and cut them into slices.

2. Cut the chicken into cubes.

3. Heat the oil in the wok and then put the garlic to sauté.

4. Add the mushrooms and a little salt and cook for 10 minutes, stirring frequently.

5. Add the chicken and cook for another 5 minutes.

6. Then add the bamboo, ½ glass of water and continue cooking for another 5 minutes.

7. Dissolve the potato starch in a cup with the soy sauce and then pour it into the wok.

8. Cook until the sauce thickens and then switch off.

9. Divide the chicken, bamboo and mushrooms between two plates and serve.

Chow Mein

Chinese Recipes

Preapering	Servings	Cooking	Calories
20 Minutes	2 People	20 Minutes	364

Ingredients:

- 3.5 oz of chicken breast
- 3.5 oz of bok choy
- 1 minced garlic clove
- ½ carrot
- 1 spring onion
- 3.5 oz of noodles
- ½ cup bean sprouts
- 2 tbsp of chicken broth
- 1 tbsp of cornstarch
- 1 tbsp of soy sauce
- 2 tsp of oyster sauce
- 2 tsp of mirin
- 2 tsp of brown sugar
- Sesame seed oil to taste
- White pepper to taste

Nutritional Values:

Carb: 76 Gr.   Proteins: 15 Gr.

Fats: 4 Gr.   Sugars: 2 Gr.

Sodium: 312 Mg.

Steps for Cooking:

1. Cut the chicken breast into strips.

2. Wash the cabbage and cut the leaves into strips.

3. Peel the carrot and cut it into sticks.

4. Place the cornstarch and soy sauce in a bowl, then add the oyster sauce, mirin, sugar, 1 tbsp sesame oil, and white pepper.

5. Add the chicken and leave to marinate for 10 minutes.

6. Put the noodles to cook in boiling salted water for 5 minutes.

7. Heat the oil in the wok, add the garlic and sauté for 2 minutes.

8. Add the chicken and marinade and sauté for a couple of minutes.

9. Now add the cabbage, carrot and spring onion.

10. Sauté for 5 minutes and then add the drained noodles.

11. Sauté for 2 minutes without ever ceasing to mix. Finally, add the bean sprouts, mix well and switch off. Serve.

Kung Pao Chicken

Chinese Recipes

Preapering	Servings	Cooking	Calories
20 Minutes	2 People	20 Minutes	379

Ingredients:

- 1.7 oz of yellow and red peppers
- 1.7 oz of cashews
- 7 oz of chicken breast
- ½ chopped of dry hot pepper
- 1 tsp of Chili sauce
- 1 tbsp of sesame seed oil
- 7 Sichuan peppercorns
- 1 tbsp of chopped spring onion
- Seed oil to taste
- 2 tbsp of water
- Salt to taste
- 2 tbsp of rice wine
- 1 tsp of potato starch
- 1 tsp of brown sugar
- 1 tsp of rice vinegar
- 1 tbsp of chicken broth
- 1 tsp of oyster sauce
- 1 minced garlic clove

Nutritional Values:

Carb:	22 Gr.	Proteins:	39 Gr.
Fats:	9 Gr.	Sugars:	10 Gr.
Sodium:			240 Mg.

Steps for Cooking:

1. Cut the chicken into cubes and put it in a bowl.

2. Add a pinch of salt, rice wine, water, sugar and toasted sesame oil to the chicken.

3. Mix well, cover with a sheet of plastic wrap and leave to rest in the fridge for 20 minutes.

4. Now prepare the sauce. Mix the soy sauce, chicken broth, vinegar, oyster sauce, sugar and a pinch of salt in a bowl.

5. Dissolve the potato starch in two tablespoons of water and add it to the sauce, mix well and set aside.

6. Wash the peppers, remove the seeds and cut them into strips.

7. Heat the seed oil in the wok, then add the cashews, brown them for 2 minutes, then remove them from the wok and set aside.

8. Add more oil and Sichuan pepper, sauté it for a few seconds and then remove it and set aside.

9. Now add the garlic and chili. Sauté for 1 minute and then add the chicken. Stir and cook for 2 minutes then add the peppers, spring onion and cashews.

10. Cook for 3 minutes, then add the sauce. Cook for another 5 minutes, stirring frequently and then switch off.

Marinated Salmon Fillet With Bok Choy

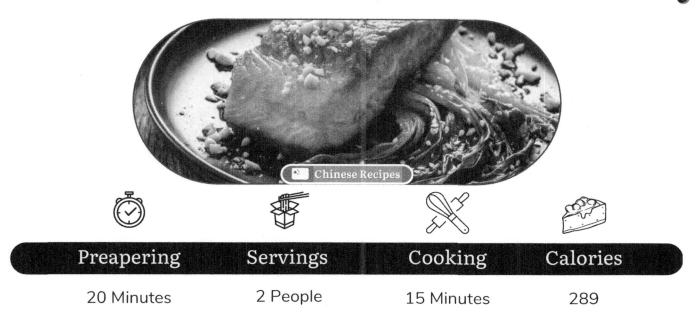

Chinese Recipes

Preapering	Servings	Cooking	Calories
20 Minutes	2 People	15 Minutes	289

Ingredients:

- 2 salmon fillets
- 1/3 cup sweet soy sauce
- 4 tbsp of water
- 2 tsp of brown sugar
- 2 tsp of dark honey
- 1 tsp of fresh ginger
- 1 clove of garlic
- Black pepper in grains
- Extra virgin olive oil to taste
- 2 bok choy
- Toasted mixed seeds to taste

Nutritional Values:

Carb:	14 Gr.
Sugars:	6 Gr.
Proteins:	28 Gr.
Fats:	14 Gr.
Sodium:	350 Mg.

Steps for Cooking:

1. In a large, shallow bowl, dissolve the sugar and honey in the soy sauce mixed with the water.

2. Crush the garlic and put it in the bowl. Add the minced ginger and black peppercorns.

3. Place the salmon cut into cubes on top and mix well. Leave to marinate for 2 hours by covering it with plastic wrap and turning the salmon from time to time.

4. Meanwhile, remove the stem from the bok choi and blanch the leaves quickly in boiling salted water. Drain them and keep them aside.

5. Put the olive oil in the wok and let it heat up. Add the bok choi and sauté for 4 minutes.

6. Add the salmon and marinade and cook for another 4 minutes.

7. Put the salmon, the bok choi and the cooking juices on two plates, sprinkle with the mixed seeds and serve.

Noodle Soup

Chinese Recipes

Preapering	Servings	Cooking	Calories
15 Minutes	2 People	20 Minutes	255

Ingredients:

- 1 small spring onion
- 1.4 oz of shitake mushrooms
- ½ tbsp peanut oil
- 4 cups of chicken broth
- 1 star anise
- 1 tsp of crushed red pepper
- ½ tsp ground cinnamon
- 1.7 oz of rice noodles
- 1 tbsp soy sauce
- ½ lime

Nutritional Values:

Carb:	36 Gr.
Sugars:	6 Gr.
Proteins:	3 Gr.
Fats:	5 Gr.
Sodium:	296 Mg.

Steps for Cooking:

1. Wash the spring onions and cut both the white and green parts into slices.

2. Clean the shitake mushrooms and cut them into strips.

3. Heat the oil in the wok and add the mushrooms and the white part of the spring onion.

4. Sauté for a few minutes, stirring constantly and then add the broth, cinnamon and aniseed and bring to a boil.

5. Let it boil for 5 minutes, and then add the noodles. Leave to soften for 8 minutes, and add the green part of the spring onions and the chili pepper.

6. Mix well, let it flavor for a few seconds and then switch off.

7. Divide the noodles, shitake mushrooms and broth between two plates, add the sliced lime and serve.

Rice Noodles with Meat & Vegetables

Chinese Recipes

Preapering	Servings	Cooking	Calories
20 Minutes	2 People	20 Minutes	369

Ingredients:

- 3.5 oz of rice noodles
- 1.7 oz of pork loin
- 1.7 oz of zucchini
- 1.7 oz of carrots
- ½ onion
- 1 egg
- 3 tbsp sunflower oil
- Soy sauce to taste
- Salt and pepper to taste

Nutritional Values:

Carb:	46 Gr.
Sugars:	6 Gr.
Proteins:	20 Gr.
Fats:	6 Gr.
Sodium:	90 Mg.

Steps for Cooking:

1. Put the rice noodles in a bowl and let them soak for 30 minutes.

2. Cut the zucchini and carrot into thin sticks.

3. Peel the onion and cut it into small pieces.

4. Cut the pork loin into thin slices.

5. Heat the oil in the wok and sauté the onion for 5 minutes.

6. Add the meat, cook for 30 seconds then move the meat and onion to one side of the wok and add the egg.

7. Stir continuously for 30 seconds and then add the carrot and zucchini. Cook for 10 minutes.

8. Drain the rice noodles and put them in the wok. Season with salt, pepper and 2 tbsp soy sauce and sauté for 5 minutes, stirring constantly.

9. After 5 minutes, switch off, divide the rice noodles with pork and vegetables into two plates and serve.

Sauteed Bok Choi

Chinese Recipes

Preapering	Servings	Cooking	Calories
20 Minutes	2 People	10 Minutes	42

Ingredients:

- 7 oz of bok choi
- 1 clove of garlic
- 2 tsp of oyster sauce
- Sesame seeds to taste
- 1 tbsp of peanut oil
- 2 tsp of chopped fresh ginger
- 1 tsp of salt
- 1 tsp of black pepper

Nutritional Values:

Carb:	12 Gr.
Sugars:	6 Gr.
Proteins:	4 Gr.
Fats:	5 Gr.
Sodium:	160 Mg.

Steps for Cooking:

1. Remove the stem from the bok choi, remove the leaves and wash them.

2. Also, wash the stem and then divide it into four parts.

3. Peel the garlic and chop it finely.

4. Put the wok to heat and, when it is hot enough, add the oil and let it heat.

5. Then add the garlic, ginger and bok choi stem and mix well.

6. Then pour the leaves and sauté for 2 minutes.

7. Now add salt, pepper and oyster sauce. Cook for 8 minutes, stirring frequently.

8. After 8 minutes, switch off and sprinkle with sesame seeds.

9. You can now divide the bok choi and the cooking liquid into two plates and serve.

Sauteed Tofu, Peppers & Bok Choy

Chinese Recipes

Preapering	Servings	Cooking	Calories
20 Minutes	2 People	8 Minutes	144

Ingredients:

- 7 oz of bok choi
- 1 clove of garlic
- 2 tsp of oyster sauce
- Sesame seeds to taste
- 1 tbsp of peanut oil
- 2 tsp of chopped fresh ginger
- 1 tsp of salt
- 1 tsp of black pepper

Nutritional Values:

Carb:	15 Gr.
Sugars:	5 Gr.
Proteins:	18 Gr.
Fats:	3 Gr.
Sodium:	180 Mg.

Steps for Cooking:

1. Tofu should be cut into cubes and marinated for ten minutes in a bowl with soy sauce, rice vinegar, and sesame oil.

2. The onion should be peeled and sliced into wedges. The carrots should be peeled and sliced into sticks. Remove the seeds, wash, and cut the pepper into strips after cutting it in half.

3. Wash, separate, and cut the Chinese cabbage's leaves into strips.

4. Crush and peel the garlic. Chili should be cut into rings.

5. The chili pepper, garlic, and onions are added to the wok and are sautéed for a short time.

6. Add the carrots, cabbage, and pepper at this point, and sauté for 3 minutes while stirring constantly.

7. After removing the tofu from the marinade and immediately browning it on all sides over high heat in a separate skillet with some sesame oil.

8. After 8 minutes, switch off and sprinkle with sesame seeds.The tofu and marinade should now be added to the wok. 3 minutes of sautéing followed by turning off.

9. Serve the tofu, vegetables, and sauce that has accumulated on the wok's bottom between two dishes.

Scallops with Ginger

Chinese Recipes

Preapering	Servings	Cooking	Calories
20 Minutes	2 People	15 Minutes	261

Ingredients:

- 7 oz of pre-cleaned scallops
- 2 tsp of peanut oil
- 1 tsp of minced ginger
- 1/2 cup of diced carrots
- 2 tsp of soy sauce
- Salt to taste
- 1 tsp of cornstarch
- 2 tbsp of spring onions cut into rings
- 1 cup of already-cooked rice

Nutritional Values:

Carb:	12 Gr.
Sugars:	10 Gr.
Proteins:	16 Gr.
Fats:	7 Gr.
Sodium:	697 Mg.

Steps for Cooking:

1. Put the oil in the wok and let it heat up.

2. Add the ginger and sauté for 30 seconds.

3. Now put the carrots and cook for 2 minutes.

4. Now add the scallops, which you have rinsed under running water, and cook for 3 minutes.

5. Now add the soy sauce, salt and cornstarch and cook until the sauce thickens.

6. Divide the rice between two plates, add the scallops, sprinkle with the sauce and the vegetables left in the wok and serve.

Soy Chicken

Chinese Recipes

Preapering	Servings	Cooking	Calories
20 Minutes	2 People	15 Minutes	402

Ingredients:

- 10.5 oz of chicken breast
- 2 tbsp of bean sprouts
- 2 tbsp of soy sauce
- 2 tsp of oyster sauce
- ½ tsp of cornstarch
- 1 minced garlic clove
- 1 spring onion
- Sesame seed oil to taste
- Salt and pepper to taste

Nutritional Values:

Carb:	5 Gr.
Sugars:	2 Gr.
Proteins:	41 Gr.
Fats:	10 Gr.
Sodium:	256 Mg.

Steps for Cooking:

1. Wash the onion and cut it into slices.

2. Cut the chicken into cubes.

3. Heat the sesame seed oil in the wok and put the garlic and the white part of the spring onion to sauté for 5 minutes.

4. Now add the chicken and cook for 5 minutes.

5. Add the soy sauce, mix and cook for 2 minutes.

6. Dissolve the cornstarch in a cup full of water and pour it into the wok.

7. Also, add the bean sprouts and continue cooking for another two minutes, stirring frequently. Season with salt and pepper and turn off.

8. Sprinkle with the green part of the spring onion, divide the chicken and sauce between two plates and serve.

Soy Noodles with Vegetables

Chinese Recipes

Preapering	Servings	Cooking	Calories
20 Minutes	2 People	20 Minutes	256

Ingredients:

- 3.5 oz of soy noodles
- 1.7 oz of zucchini
- 1 small carrot
- 1 tbsp of chopped onion
- 2 tbsp of soy sauce
- 1 tsp of peanut oil
- 1 tbsp of sliced red bell pepper
- 1 tsp of sesame seed oil
- 2 tsp of sunflower oil

Nutritional Values:

Carb:	44 Gr.
Sugars:	12 Gr.
Proteins:	3 Gr.
Fats:	9 Gr.
Sodium:	870 Mg.

Steps for Cooking:

1. Put the soy noodles in a bowl full of water and leave them to soak for 30 minutes.

2. In the meantime, wash the zucchini and cut it into sticks.

3. Peel the carrot, wash it and cut it into sticks.

4. Pour the sunflower oil into the wok and heat it.

5. Then add the onion, carrot, zucchini and pepper and sauté for 10 minutes.

6. At this point, pour ½ cup of water and bring to a boil.

7. Pour the drained soy noodles and mix well.

8. Add the soy sauce, and salt and pepper if needed and mix again.

9. Cook for 5 minutes, then add the sesame oil and peanut oil.

10. Stir continuously, cook for 2 minutes then switch off.

11. Divide the soy noodles between two plates and serve.

Spicy Shrimp

Chinese Recipes

Preapering	Servings	Cooking	Calories
25 Minutes	2 People	10 Minutes	288

Ingredients:

- 7 oz of shrimp
- ½ small green pepper
- 1 tbsp of tomato sauce
- 1 tsp of cornstarch
- ½ small red pepper
- ½ shallot
- 1 tbsp of chili sauce
- 2 tbsp of roasted cashews
- Salt to taste
- Peanut oil to taste

Nutritional Values:

Carb:	6 Gr.
Sugars:	1 Gr.
Proteins:	26 Gr.
Fats:	7 Gr.
Sodium:	190 Mg.

Steps for Cooking:

1. Remove the head, tail and carapace and intestinal filament from the shrimp, wash them and keep them aside.

2. Wash the peppers and cut them into strips.

3. Peel the shallot and cut it into slices.

4. Heat the peanut oil in the wok and then add the prawns. Sauté for 3 minutes, then remove them with a slotted spoon and set aside.

5. Now add the peppers and onion and sauté for 3 minutes.

6. After 3 minutes, add the tomato sauce and chili sauce and put the shrimp back.

7. Stir and then add the cornstarch dissolved in ½ glass of water.

8. Cook for a few minutes, the time necessary for the sauce to thicken and then add the cashews.

9. Mix well, cook for 1 minute and then switch off.

10. Divide the shrimp and hot sauce between two plates and serve.

Suan Tian Tu Dou Si: Hot & Spicy Potatoes

Chinese Recipes

Preapering	Servings	Cooking	Calories
25 Minutes	2 People	20 Minutes	176

Ingredients:

- 10.5 oz of potatoes
- 2 cloves of minced garlic
- 1 spring onion
- 2 tsp of rice vinegar
- Chopped pepper to taste
- Chopped ginger to taste
- Seed oil to taste
- Salt to taste

Nutritional Values:

Carb:	9 Gr.
Sugars:	2 Gr.
Proteins:	3 Gr.
Fats:	10 Gr.
Sodium:	895 Mg.

Steps for Cooking:

1. Peel the potatoes and cut them into pickled sticks. Put them in a bowl covered with water.

2. Heat some vegetable oil in the wok and let it heat up. Add the garlic and chili and sauté for 2 minutes.

3. Add the potatoes, mix well and cook for 10 minutes, stirring constantly.

4. Season with salt, add the vinegar and the green part of the onion cut into slices.

5. Continue cooking for another 5 minutes.

6. Once cooked, put the potatoes in a bowl, bring them to the table and serve.

Sweet & Sour Pork

Chinese Recipes

Preapering	Servings	Cooking	Calories
25 Minutes	2 People	12 Minutes	370

Ingredients:

- 8.8 oz of pork loin
- 1 green pepper
- 1 tbsp of cornstarch
- 1 tbsp of soy sauce
- 1 tsp of crushed red pepper
- 2 tsp of brown sugar
- 1 tbsp of rice vinegar
- Salt and pepper to taste
- Seed oil to taste

Nutritional Values:

Carb:	13 Gr.
Sugars:	5 Gr.
Proteins:	27 Gr.
Fats:	16 Gr.
Sodium:	304 Mg.

Steps for Cooking:

1. Cut the pork loin into cubes.

2. Wash the pepper, cut it into cubes and put it in a bowl, together with the soy sauce and cornstarch.

3. Heat the seed oil in the wok and brown the pork over high heat, stirring constantly for 5 minutes, then remove it from the wok and set aside.

4. Now add the chili pepper and brown for 1 minute, then add the pepper mixture and brown for about 40 seconds, stirring constantly.

5. Add the meat again and mix well for a few seconds.

6. Finally, add the sugar and vinegar, mix well and cook for 1 minute.

7. Once cooked, divide the pork and sweet and sour sauce between two plates and serve.

Sweet & Sour Tofu

Chinese Recipes

Preapering	Servings	Cooking	Calories
20 Minutes	2 People	22 Minutes	357

Ingredients:

- 1.7 oz of yellow peppers
- 1 small red onion
- 5.2 oz of tofu
- ½ glass of sweet and sour sauce
- ½ glass of water
- 2 tbsp of soy sauce
- 1 tbsp of chicken broth
- 1 tsp of brown sugar
- 1 tsp of oyster sauce
- 1 tsp of cornstarch
- Peanut oil to taste

Nutritional Values:

Carb:	33 Gr.
Sugars:	5 Gr.
Proteins:	16 Gr.
Fats:	10 Gr.
Sodium:	395 Mg.

Steps for Cooking:

1. Take the tofu, put it on a cutting board and cut it into cubes.

2. Peel the onion and then divide it into 8 pieces.

3. Wash the peppers and cut them into strips.

4. Put the vegetable oil in the wok and let it heat. Pour in the tofu and let it brown for 5 minutes.

5. Remove the tofu with a slotted spoon and set aside.

6. Heat a little more oil in the wok and add the onion and peppers.

7. Cook for 10 minutes, remove the onion and peppers from the wok and add the soy sauce, chicken broth, sugar, oyster sauce and cornstarch dissolved in a cup of cold water.

8. Stir and cook for 5 minutes and then add the tofu and vegetables.

9. Mix for 30 seconds and then turn off.

10. Divide the sweet and sour tofu between two plates and serve.

Tofu Lo Mein

Chinese Recipes

Preapering	Servings	Cooking	Calories
20 Minutes	2 People	25 Minutes	230

Ingredients:

- 7.7 oz of tofu
- 1 tbsp of seed oil
- 1 glass of water
- 1.5 oz of noodles
- 1 small potato
- 3.5 oz of bok choy
- 1 carrot
- 3.5 oz of green beans
- 1 tbsp soy sauce

Nutritional Values:

Carb:	32 Gr.
Sugars:	8 Gr.
Proteins:	10 Gr.
Fats:	7 Gr.
Sodium:	315 Mg.

Steps for Cooking:

1. Peel the potato, wash it and cut it into cubes.

2. Peel the carrot and cut it into thin sticks.

3. Wash the Chinese cabbage leaves and cut them into small pieces.

4. Drain the tofu, pat it dry with a paper towel and cut it into cubes.

5. Heat the oil in the wok and add the tofu. Cook until golden brown, stirring frequently to prevent burning.

6. Remove the tofu and put the vegetables to cook together with the glass of water. Cook for 15 minutes or until vegetables is tender.

7. Meanwhile, put the water in a pot and bring it to a boil.

8. Pour the noodles and cook for 2 minutes. After 2 minutes, drain the noodles.

9. Put the noodles and tofu in the wok and add the soy sauce. Mix well, let it infuse and then switch it off.

10. Divide the noodles, vegetables and cooking liquid between two plates and serve.

Chicken Ramen

Chinese Recipes

Preapering	Servings	Cooking	Calories
25 Minutes	2 People	15 Minutes	386

Ingredients:

- 4.9 oz of noodles
- 8.8 oz of chicken breast
- 1 tbsp of soy sauce
- 2 tsp of sesame seeds
- 2 tsp of grated fresh ginger
- 1 tsp of brown sugar
- 1 fresh spring onion
- ½ chopped fresh chili
- 2 cups of chicken broth
- 1 egg
- Sesame seed oil to taste

Nutritional Values:

Carb:	53 Gr.
Sugars:	10 Gr.
Proteins:	0 Gr.
Fats:	14 Gr.
Sodium:	530 Mg.

Steps for Cooking:

1. Wash the spring onion and cut the white part into rounds.

2. Put the egg in a saucepan covered with water and bring it to a boil. Continue cooking for 9 minutes and switch off. Run the eggs under cold water and let them cool.

3. Cut the chicken into strips and put it to sauté in the wok where you heated a little sesame seed oil.

4. Add the soy sauce, fresh ginger, spring onion and sugar and cook for 5 minutes.

5. Bring the chicken broth to a boil and then put the noodles to cook for 5 minutes.

6. After 5 minutes, drain the noodles and place them in two bowls. Add the chicken and then pour the broth from the noodles.

7. Peel the egg, cut it in half and place each half in the bowls and serve.

Fried Tofu in Broth

Chinese Recipes

Preapering	Servings	Cooking	Calories
20 Minutes	2 People	10 Minutes	271

Ingredients:

- 7 oz of tofu
- 1 tbsp of cornstarch
- 3.5 oz of dashi broth
- 1 tbsp of soy sauce
- 1 tbsp of mirin
- 1 tbsp of grated daikon
- 2 tsp of chopped fresh ginger
- 1 small onion
- 1 tsp of katsuobushi
- Soybean oil to taste

Nutritional Values:

Carb:	11 Gr.
Sugars:	3 Gr.
Proteins:	18 Gr.
Fats:	20 Gr.
Sodium:	160 Mg.

Steps for Cooking:

1. Using a weight on the cutting board at the top, press the tofu between two cutting boards. Give the tofu 30 minutes to rest.

2. Take the tofu and divide it into 8 equal pieces once 30 minutes have passed. Place the tofu chunks on top of the cornstarch in a plate.

3. The tofu chunks are added to a wok that has been heated with soybean oil. The tofu chunks should be perfectly browned before being removed from the pan and placed on a plate to cool.

4. In the meantime, combine the broth, soy sauce, and mirin in a pot and heat until boiling.

5. Place the tofu pieces in two bowls and top each with some daikon and ginger.

6. After adding the katsuobushi that have been sliced into flakes, pour the soup into the bowls and serve.

Kabocha Miso Soup

Chinese Recipes

Preapering	Servings	Cooking	Calories
20 Minutes	2 People	20 Minutes	171

Ingredients:

- 2 tbsp of toasted white sesame seeds
- 7 oz of pumpkin pulp
- 1 tbsp of soy sauce
- 2 cups of water
- 1.7 oz of mushrooms
- 2 tbsp of Japanese miso or dashi miso

Nutritional Values:

Carb:	11 Gr.
Sugars:	4 Gr.
Proteins:	6 Gr.
Fats:	4 Gr.
Sodium:	458 Mg.

Steps for Cooking:

1. Wash the pumpkin and cut it into cubes.

2. Put the sesame seeds in a non-stick pan and toast them for a couple of minutes.

3. Put the squash in the wok, add the water and bring to a boil.

4. Lower the heat, add the soy sauce and cook for another 15 minutes.

5. In the meantime, clean the mushrooms well, cut them into slices and, after 15 minutes, put them in the wok with the pumpkin.

6. Turn off and add the miso and sesame seeds and mix well.

7. Divide the kabocha miso soup between two bowls and serve.

Kara Age: Japanese fried chicken

Chinese Recipes

Preapering	Servings	Cooking	Calories
25 Minutes	2 People	15 Minutes	392

Ingredients:

- 10.5 oz of chicken
- 1 slice of apple
- 1 tsp of fresh minced ginger
- 1 tbsp of sake
- 1 tbsp of soy sauce
- ½ tsp salt
- 2 tbsp of potato starch
- 2 tbsp of flour
- Peanut oil to taste

Nutritional Values:

Carb:	11 Gr.
Sugars:	4 Gr.
Proteins:	6 Gr.
Fats:	4 Gr.
Sodium:	458 Mg.

Steps for Cooking:

1. Remove the bones from the chicken, cut them into cubes and put it in a bowl.

2. Grate the apple and place it in the bowl with the chicken.

3. Add the sake, soy sauce and salt: mix everything well.

4. Cover the bowl with plastic wrap making it adhere well to prevent air from entering and leave it to rest in the fridge for at least 30 minutes.

5. After 30 minutes, take the chicken from the fridge, put the flour and starch on a plate and flour the chicken pieces.

6. Pour the peanut oil into the wok and heat well. Then delicately dip the chicken nuggets and cook them over high heat until they are golden brown.

7. Remove the chicken pieces from the wok and let the excess oil absorb on a paper towel.

8. Put the chicken nuggets in a bowl, bring them to the table and serve accompanied with a slightly spicy sweet and sour sauce.

Miso Crab Stock (Kanijiru)

Chinese Recipes

Preapering	Servings	Cooking	Calories
20 Minutes	2 People	15 Minutes	231

Ingredients:

- 1 crab
- ½ leek
- 2 tbsp miso
- 3 cups of water

Nutritional Values:

Carb:	6 Gr.
Sugars:	3 Gr.
Proteins:	22 Gr.
Fats:	6 Gr.
Sodium:	400 Mg.

Steps for Cooking:

1. Clean the crab. Cut it in half, remove the triangular part of the lower abdomen side by hand, then rinse with running water.

2. Wash the leek and cut it into thin slices.

3. Put the water in the wok and bring it to a boil. Now dip the crab pieces into the wok.

4. Cook for a few minutes and with a slotted spoon remove the foam and the white pieces that emerge on the surface.

5. Now add the sliced leek. Cook for 5 minutes then add the miso. Melt the miso, stirring constantly and heat the broth again without bringing it to a boil.

6. Now switch off, divide the crab with the broth into two bowls and serve.

Nikujaga, Beef & Potato Stew

Chinese Recipes

Preapering	Servings	Cooking	Calories
20 Minutes	2 People	15 Minutes	481

Ingredients:

- 14 oz of potatoes
- 3.5 oz of beef tenderloin
- ½ onion
- 1 cup of water
- 2 tbsp of brown sugar
- 2 tbsp of soy sauce
- 1 carrot

Nutritional Values:

Carb:	24 Gr.
Sugars:	8 Gr.
Proteins:	28 Gr.
Fats:	6 Gr.
Sodium:	400 Mg.

Steps for Cooking:

1. Peel the potatoes, cut them into 6 pieces and wash them and then immerse them in a bowl with clean water for 10 minutes.

2. Peel the onion and cut it into thin slices. Also, cut the beef tenderloin into thin slices.

3. Put the water in the wok and bring it to a boil. Then add the potatoes and onion and cook for 3 minutes.

4. After 3 minutes, add half the sugar and cook over low heat for another 2 minutes.

5. Add half of the soy sauce, and the beef a little at a time, remembering to stir often to distribute the flavor evenly.

6. When the meat has started to change color, add the rest of the sugar and the rest of the soy sauce.

7. Reduce the heat, add the lid to the wok and cook for another 10 minutes.

8. Put the meat and potatoes in two bowls and tilt the wok to thicken the gravy.

9. Pour the gravy over the meat and potatoes and serve.

Salmon Udon

Chinese Recipes

Preapering	Servings	Cooking	Calories
20 Minutes	2 People	15 Minutes	360

Ingredients:

- 7 oz of salmon
- 1 tbsp of soy sauce
- 1 tbsp of sake
- 2 tbsp of mirin
- 1 tsp of brown sugar
- 1 tsp of minced ginger
- 1 minced garlic clove
- 1 tbsp of peanut oil
- 3.5 oz of udon
- 2 tbsp of bean sprouts
- 1 tbsp of sesame seeds

Nutritional Values:

Carb:	52 Gr.
Sugars:	30 Gr.
Proteins:	26 Gr.
Fats:	7 Gr.
Sodium:	609 Mg.

Steps for Cooking:

1. Cut the salmon into thin slices and put them on a plate.

2. Mix the soy sauce, sake, mirin, sugar, ginger and minced garlic in a bowl. Pour over the salmon and leave to marinate for 30 minutes.

3. Cook the udon in boiling salted water for 5 minutes, then drain and set aside.

4. Heat the seed oil in the wok and put the garlic to brown without letting it burn.

5. Add the salmon slices and the marinade and sauté for 2 minutes.

6. Pour the udon and sauté for 3 minutes, stirring constantly.

7. Finally, add the bean sprouts and sesame seeds and mix well.

8. Turn off the stove, divide the udon and salmon between two plates and serve.

Sauteed Udon with Shrimp & Vegetables

Chinese Recipes

Preapering	Servings	Cooking	Calories
25 Minutes	2 People	20 Minutes	318

Ingredients:

- 3.5 oz of udon
- 6 tbsp of soy sauce
- 4 tbsp of mirin
- 2 tsp of dashi
- 2tbsp of peanut oil
- 1 carrot
- 1 zucchini
- Soybeans to taste
- 1 savoy cabbage leaf
- 7 oz of shrimp
- 6 shitake mushrooms

Nutritional Values:

Carb:	48 Gr.
Sugars:	30 Gr.
Proteins:	33 Gr.
Fats:	5 Gr.
Sodium:	410 Mg.

Steps for Cooking:

1. Put water and salt in a saucepan and bring to a boil. Cook the udon for 5 minutes and then drain and set aside.

2. Peel the carrot and cut it into sticks. Wash the zucchini and cut it into sticks.

3. Clean the mushrooms well and cut them into slices.

4. Wash the cabbage leaf and cut it into small pieces.

5. Shell the shrimp, remove the intestinal filament and wash them.

6. Heat the oil in the wok and sauté the vegetables for 10 minutes.

7. Then add the shrimp and mirin and cook for 3 minutes.

8. Add the dashi and soy sauce and mix well.

9. Now add the udon, mix and cook until everything is well incorporated.

10. Finally, add the bean sprouts, mix once more and switch off.

11. Divide the udon, prawns and vegetables between two plates and serve.

Shrimp in Teriyaki Sauce

Chinese Recipes

Preapering	Servings	Cooking	Calories
20 Minutes	2 People	5 Minutes	243

Ingredients:

- 7 oz of shrimp
- 2 tbsp of soy sauce
- 2 tbsp of water
- 2 tsp of honey
- 1 tsp of cornstarch
- 2 tbsp of mirin
- 2 tbsp of sake
- Chopped ginger to taste

Nutritional Values:

Carb:	17 Gr.
Sugars:	7 Gr.
Proteins:	28 Gr.
Fats:	7 Gr.
Sodium:	530 Mg.

Steps for Cooking:

1 Remove the head, carapace and tail from the shrimp, remove the intestinal filament and wash them.

2 Put the soy sauce, mirin, sake, honey and ginger in the wok and bring to a boil.

3 Add the cornstarch and let it thicken.

4 Now pour the shrimp, mix well and cook for 4 minutes.

5 Once cooked, switch off, divide the shrimp into two plates and serve.

Soy Spaghetti with Vegetables & Shrimp

Japanese Recipes

Preapering	Servings	Cooking	Calories
25 Minutes	2 People	15 Minutes	342

Ingredients:

- 3.5 oz of soy noodles
- 5.2 oz of shrimp
- 1 red pepper
- 1 yellow pepper
- 1 fresh spring onion
- 1 clove of garlic
- 1 tsp of brown sugar
- 2 tbsp of sunflower oil
- 2 tbsp of soy sauce
- 1 tsp of fresh ginger
- 1 tsp of rice vinegar
- Vegetable broth to taste
- ½ orange

Nutritional Values:

Carb:	54 Gr.
Sugars:	22 Gr.
Proteins:	11 Gr.
Fats:	4 Gr.
Sodium:	915 Mg.

Steps for Cooking:

1. Wash the onion and cut it into strips. Peel the ginger and cut it into small pieces.
2. Remove the stalk and seeds from the peppers, wash them and cut them into sticks.
3. Peel the prawns. Score the back of the prawns with a small knife and, pulling gently, remove the black thread.
4. Pour the seed oil into the wok and let it heat up.
5. Crush the garlic clove and put it in the wok. Add the ginger and spring onion.
6. Cook for two minutes and then add the peppers.
7. Cook for 2 minutes, blend them with a spoonful of rice vinegar, then add the brown sugar and finally the soy sauce.
8. Now add the filtered orange juice and continue cooking for another 2 minutes.
9. Now add the prawns, mix well and cook for another 3 minutes.
10. Bring the water and a little salt to a boil in a saucepan and boil the soy spaghetti for a maximum of two minutes with the lid on.
11. Drain the soy noodles, pass them under cold water and then put them in the wok. Mix well and cook for 1 minute.
12. Turn off the heat, put the soy spaghetti, the vegetables, the prawns and the cooking juices on two plates and serve.

Tatsutaage: Fried Mackerel

Japanese Recipes

Preapering	Servings	Cooking	Calories
20 Minutes	2 People	10 Minutes	336

Ingredients:

- 7 oz filleted mackerel
- 1 tbsp of soy sauce
- 1 tbsp of mirin
- 1 tbsp of sake
- 1 tsp of minced ginger
- 1 tsp of potato starch
- Peanut oil to taste

Nutritional Values:

Carb:	8 Gr.
Sugars:	1 Gr.
Proteins:	36 Gr.
Fats:	14 Gr.
Sodium:	390 Mg.

Steps for Cooking:

1. Wash the mackerel fillets and cut them into 4 parts. Put the mackerel pieces in a bowl.

2. Put ginger, soy sauce, mirin, and sake in another bowl and mix well.

3. Pour the sauce over the mackerel pieces, refrigerate and marinate for 3 hours.

4. Shake the container during the marinade so that all the mackerel pieces season evenly.

5. Heat the oil for frying in the wok and, when it is hot, dip the mackerel pieces and cook them for 4 minutes on each side.

6. Remove the mackerel and add the marinade and potato starch. Mix well and thicken the sauce, then switch off.

7. Divide the mackerel pieces between two plates, sprinkle with the sauce and serve.

Teppanyaki

Japanese Recipes

Preapering	Servings	Cooking	Calories
25 Minutes	2 People	20 Minutes	435

Ingredients:

- 7 oz of beef tenderloin
- 1 eggplant
- 1.7 oz of mushrooms
- 1.7 oz of green beans
- 1.7 oz of yellow squash
- ½ red pepper
- 2 tbsp of soy sauce
- 1 tbsp of seed oil
- 3.5 oz of bamboo shoots
- 1 spring onion
- Salt and pepper to taste

Nutritional Values:

Carb:	20 Gr.
Sugars:	12 Gr.
Proteins:	26 Gr.
Fats:	10 Gr.
Sodium:	480 Mg.

Steps for Cooking:

1. Cut the beef tenderloin into thin slices, place them in a baking dish and season with salt and pepper.

2. Remove the ends of the eggplant and cut them into thin slices diagonally.

3. Cut the pumpkin and pepper into slices.

4. Trim the green beans, wash them and cut them into 3 parts.

5. Remove the green part from the spring onions and cut them into slices.

6. Clean the mushrooms well and then cut them into slices.

7. Heat the oil in the wok and sauté the vegetables for 10 minutes.

8. Add the meat and soy sauce and sauté for another 5 minutes.

9. Add the bamboo shoots, cook for 2 minutes and switch off.

10. Divide the meat and vegetables between two plates and serve.

Teriyaki Chicken

Japanese Recipes

Preapering	Servings	Cooking	Calories
20 Minutes	2 People	10 Minutes	289

Ingredients:

- 14 oz of chicken breast
- Peanut oil to taste
- 1 tbsp of toasted sesame seeds
- 4 tbsp of soy sauce
- 1 tbsp of mirin
- 2 tsp of brown sugar
- 1 tbsp of sake
- The green part of a spring onion

Nutritional Values:

Carb:	16 Gr.
Sugars:	6 Gr.
Proteins:	36 Gr.
Fats:	10 Gr.
Sodium:	383 Mg.

Steps for Cooking:

1. Wash the green part of the spring onion and cut it into slices.

2. Cut the chicken into cubes.

3. Put the soy sauce, mirin, sake and brown sugar into the wok and bring to a boil, stirring constantly.

4. Let the sauce thicken for a couple of minutes and then add the chicken.

5. Sauté for 5 minutes, or until chicken is cooked through.

6. Now add the spring onion and sesame seeds and mix well.

7. Turn off the stove, divide the teriyaki chicken between two plates and serve.

Teriyaki Salmon

Japanese Recipes

Preapering	Servings	Cooking	Calories
20 Minutes	2 People	10 Minutes	337

Ingredients:

- 2 salmon fillets 7 oz
- 2 tbsp of soy sauce
- 2 tbsp of sake
- 2 tbsp of mirin
- 1 tsp of brown sugar
- Peanut oil to taste

Nutritional Values:

Carb:	18 Gr.
Sugars:	7 Gr.
Proteins:	43 Gr.
Fats:	14 Gr.
Sodium:	612 Mg.

Steps for Cooking:

1. Wash the salmon fillets and pat them dry with a paper towel.

2. Prepare the teriyaki sauce. In a bowl, put the soy sauce, wine, mirin and sugar, and mix well.

3. Dip the salmon slices in the teriyaki sauce, and leave to marinate in the fridge for 4 hours.

4. Heat a little seed oil in the wok, and when it's hot, put the salmon, skin side down, to cook.

5. Cook for 3 minutes and then turn the salmon and continue cooking for 6 minutes.

6. Now add the marinade and cook for another 3 minutes.

7. Switch off, divide the salmon between two plates, sprinkle with the sauce and serve.

Tofu Miso Soup

Japanese Recipes

Preapering	Servings	Cooking	Calories
15 Minutes	2 People	10 Minutes	279

Ingredients:

- ½ onion
- 1 carrot
- ½ daikon
- 1 stalk of celery
- 1 small leek
- 2 tbsp of seed oil
- 1 sheet of kombu seaweed
- 3.5 oz of tofu
- 1 tbsp of miso
- 1 tbsp of chopped parsley

Nutritional Values:

Carb:	21 Gr.
Sugars:	6 Gr.
Proteins:	16 Gr.
Fats:	4 Gr.
Sodium:	1058 Mg.

Steps for Cooking:

1. Peel the onion and carrot and then cut them into cubes.

2. Wash the daikon and cut it into cubes. Wash the celery and then chop it.

3. Heat the oil in the wok and then add the vegetables. Cook for 5 minutes.

4. Meanwhile, carefully wash the seaweed and cut it into small pieces, then add it to the wok.

5. Now pour two cups of water and bring to a boil.

6. Lower the heat and cook for 15 minutes.

7. Cut the tofu into cubes and, after 15 minutes, put it in the wok. Cook for 10 minutes.

8. After 10 minutes, add the miso, and dilute it for 3 minutes, stirring constantly.

9. Switch off, add the parsley, mix and leave to rest for 10 minutes.

10. After 10 minutes, you can divide the tofu and miso soup into two bowls and serve.

Tofu & Sauteed Vegetables

Japanese Recipes

Preapering	Servings	Cooking	Calories
20 Minutes	2 People	25 Minutes	319

Ingredients:

- 1 small red pepper
- 1 small green pepper
- 1 Japanese eggplant
- 3.5 oz of broccoli florets
- 1 tbsp of seed oil
- 7 oz of tofu
- 1 tbsp fresh grated ginger
- 1 spring onion
- 2 tsp mixed sesame seeds
- 1 tbsp of dashi
- 2 tsp of mirin

Nutritional Values:

Carb:	21 Gr.
Sugars:	14 Gr.
Proteins:	17 Gr.
Fats:	7 Gr.
Sodium:	680 Mg.

Steps for Cooking:

1. Wash the peppers and cut them into strips. Wash the Japanese eggplant and cut it into cubes.

2. Wash the broccoli flowers and blanch them for 10 minutes in boiling salted water. After 10 minutes, drain and set aside.

3. Wash the onion and slice both the white and green parts.

4. Cut the tofu into cubes and put it in a bowl. Add the dashi, sesame seeds, ginger, spring onion and mirin and let sit for 15 minutes.

5. Meanwhile, put the seed oil in the wok and let it heat.

6. Add the aubergine and peppers and cook for 10 minutes.

7. Then add the broccoli flowers and continue cooking for another 10 minutes.

8. Season with salt and pepper and then add the tofu and the marinade.

9. Stir, cook for another 5 minutes and then switch off.

10. Divide the vegetables, tofu and the sauce that has formed during cooking between two plates and serve.

Tsukimi Udon

Japanese Recipes

Preapering	Servings	Cooking	Calories
20 Minutes	2 People	25 Minutes	378

Ingredients:

- 2 eggs
- 6 oz of udon
- 2 cups of Hondashi broth
- 2 tbsp of soy sauce
- 2 tbsp of mirin
- 1 spring onion

Nutritional Values:

Carb:	60 Gr.
Sugars:	25 Gr.
Proteins:	19 Gr.
Fats:	6 Gr.
Sodium:	720 Mg.

Steps for Cooking:

1. Fill a pot with water. Bring the water to a boil. Cook the udon following the instructions on the package. Drain and rinse the udon with cold water.

2. Put the Hondashi broth in the wok and bring it to a boil then reduce the heat to low and simmer for 10 minutes. Turn off the flame, cover it with a lid and let it rest for 5 minutes.

3. Divide the udon into two bowls.

4. Add the soy sauce and mirin to the broth, put back on the heat, bring to a boil and then reduce the heat to a minimum.

5. Break an egg into the broth and let it cook for 3 minutes. Collect the egg with a slotted spoon and carefully place it in one of the two bowls, being careful not to break the yolk.

6. Repeat the same procedure with the other egg.

7. Add the broth passed through a sieve, add the onion cut into thin slices and serve.

Yakisoba with Shrimp with Oyster Sauce

Japanese Recipes

Preapering	Servings	Cooking	Calories
20 Minutes	2 People	15 Minutes	466

Ingredients:

- 3.5 oz of Soba
- 1.7 oz of shrimp
- ½ head of bok choi
- 1 tsp of minced ginger
- 2 tsp of oyster sauce
- Sesame seed oil

Nutritional Values:

Carb:	57 Gr.
Sugars:	16 Gr.
Proteins:	24 Gr.
Fats:	12 Gr.
Sodium:	378 Mg.

Steps for Cooking:

1. Remove the stem from the bok choi, wash the leaves and then cut them into slices.

2. Shell the shrimp, remove the black filament and then wash them.

3. Boil water in a saucepan and boil the soba al dente, then drain and drain. Put them in a bowl and add a drizzle of oil to prevent the soba from sticking.

4. Put the oil in the wok and sauté the ginger. Then add the prawns and bok choi.

5. Cook for 5 minutes, then add the oyster sauce and soy sauce.

6. Sauté for 1 minute, then add the soba noodles and mix well.

7. Turn off the wok, divide the yakisoba into two plates and serve.

Yaki Udon with Chicken & Vegetables

Japanese Recipes

Preapering	Servings	Cooking	Calories
20 Minutes	2 People	15 Minutes	388

Ingredients:

- 1 red pepper
- 1 small leek
- 1 carrot
- ½ bok choi
- 5.2 oz of chicken breast
- 2 sheets of nori seaweed
- 3 tbsp of soy sauce
- 2 tsp of grated fresh ginger
- 1 and ½ tbsp sesame seed oil
- Toasted sesame seeds to taste
- 4.4 oz of udon
- 2 cups of dashi broth

Nutritional Values:

Carb:	58 Gr.
Sugars:	38 Gr.
Proteins:	34 Gr.
Fats:	7 Gr.
Sodium:	580 Mg.

Steps for Cooking:

1. Soak the nori seaweed sheets for 5 minutes, then drain and cut into strips.

2. Separate the leaves from the stem of the bok choi and cut the leaves into strips.

3. Peel the leek, carrot and pepper and then cut all the vegetables into sticks.

4. Put the oil, vegetables and ginger in the wok and cook for 10 minutes.

5. Cut the chicken into cubes and put it in the wok together with the vegetables. Sauté for a few minutes, then add 2 tbsp soy sauce, the nori seaweed and the green leaves of the bok choi.

6. Meanwhile, bring the dashi broth to a boil with the remaining soy sauce and, as soon as it boils, dip the udon in and cook.

7. When the udon are cooked, drain them from the broth and put them in the wok with the chicken and vegetables.

8. Add the sesame seeds, mix well and then switch off.

9. Now divide the udon, chicken, vegetables and cooking juices between two plates and serve.

Yaki Udon with Vegetables

Japanese Recipes

Preapering	Servings	Cooking	Calories
25 Minutes	2 People	20 Minutes	384

Ingredients:

- 7 oz of udon
- 6 shitake mushrooms
- 1 carrot
- 1 spring onion
- 3.5 oz of broccoli florets
- 3 tbsp of soy sauce
- 1 tbsp of mirin
- 2 tbsp of sesame seed oil
- Toasted sesame seeds to taste

Nutritional Values:

Carb:	58 Gr.
Sugars:	24 Gr.
Proteins:	7 Gr.
Fats:	12 Gr.
Sodium:	360 Mg.

Steps for Cooking:

1. The dried shitake mushrooms should be soaked in cold water for at least three hours before to cooking the meal.

2. Drain the mushrooms after three hours, then cook the udon for five minutes in salted boiling water before draining and reserving.

3. Cut the carrot into sticks after peeling.

4. Cut the broccoli flowers into little pieces after washing them. Slice the onion after washing it.

5. After heating up the oil in the wok, add the mushrooms and cook for 5 minutes.

6. After adding the broccoli flowers, simmer for an additional five minutes.

7. Add the carrot and spring onion now, and cook for a further five minutes.

8. Pour the udon and soy sauce after adding the mirin and allowing it to evaporate.

9. Mix thoroughly, then turn the heat off after two minutes. After adding the sesame seeds, divide the udon and vegetables onto two dishes and serve.

Bulgogi

Korean Recipes

Preapering	Servings	Cooking	Calories
15 Minutes	2 People	8 Minutes	231

Ingredients:

- 8.8 oz of sirloin steak
- 2 minced garlic cloves
- 2 tsp of minced ginger
- 1 white onion
- 1 pear
- ½ apple
- 4 tbsp of soy sauce
- 2 tsp of sesame seed oil
- 2 tsp of brown sugar
- Salt and pepper to taste
- Sesame seeds to taste

Nutritional Values:

Carb:	12 Gr.
Sugars:	8 Gr.
Proteins:	3 Gr.
Fats:	3 Gr.
Sodium:	260 Mg.

Steps for Cooking:

1. Put the garlic, ginger, sliced onion, soy sauce, brown sugar, salt, pepper and sesame seed oil in a bowl and mix.

2. Grate the pear and apple into the bowl with the marinade and mix again.

3. Cut the meat into thin slices and place it in the bowl with the marinade.

4. Place the meat in the fridge and marinate for 2 hours.

5. After 2 hours, take the meat back from the fridge and heat a little seed oil in the wok.

6. When the oil is ready, add the meat and marinade and cook for 6 minutes, stirring often.

7. Once the meat is cooked, turn it off and sprinkle it with the sesame seeds.

8. Divide the beef and the gravy between two plates and serve.

Chapche

Korean Recipes

Preapering	Servings	Cooking	Calories
20 Minutes	2 People	15 Minutes	348

Ingredients:

- 5.2 oz of beef
- 3 tbsp of soy sauce
- 2 tbsp of sesame seed oil
- 1 1/2 tbsp of sugar
- 2 tbsp of white wine
- 1 clove of garlic
- 1 tbsp of sesame seeds
- ½ white onion
- 1.7 oz of bean sprouts
- 1 oz of mushrooms
- 1 carrot
- ½ red pepper
- Peanut oil to taste
- Salt and pepper to taste

Nutritional Values:

Carb:	51 Gr.
Sugars:	8 Gr.
Proteins:	12 Gr.
Fats:	12 Gr.
Sodium:	925 Mg.

Steps for Cooking:

1. Blanch the bean sprouts in boiling salted water until they become transparent (it will take 4 minutes). Drain, dry and cut into small pieces.

2. Cut the beef into thin slices, put them in a bowl and add soy sauce, sesame oil, sugar and white wine. Mix well and let the meat marinate.

3. Peel the carrots, wash them and cut them into strips.

4. Wash the pepper and cut them into strips. Clean the mushrooms well and then cut them into slices.

5. Peel the onion and slice it thinly.

6. Put the seed oil in the wok and then add the onion. Cook for 2 minutes and add the mushrooms. Cook for another 5 minutes and add the rest of the vegetables.

7. Continue cooking for 10 minutes and finally add the beef and the marinade sauce.

8. Cook for another 3 minutes, then add the bean sprouts and cook until everything is well blended.

9. Sprinkle with the sesame seeds, then divide the Chapche between two plates and serve.

Daegu Jiri: Cod Soup

Korean Recipes

Preapering	Servings	Cooking	Calories
20 Minutes	2 People	25 Minutes	351

Ingredients:

- 8.8 oz of bean sprouts
- 10.5 oz of cod fillet
- 1.7 oz of enoki mushrooms
- 2 slices of horseradish
- 2 sheets of nori seaweed
- 4 cups of water
- 1 tsp of salt
- Chopped coriander to taste
- ½ chili pepper cut into slices
- 2 slices of lemon

Nutritional Values:

Carb:	11 Gr.
Sugars:	8 Gr.
Proteins:	47 Gr.
Fats:	13 Gr.
Sodium:	340 Mg.

Steps for Cooking:

1. Remove the roots from the bean sprouts and then wash them.

2. Cut the horseradish slices into small pieces.

3. Put the water in the wok and bring it to a boil.

4. Add the horseradish, a tsp of salt and the nori seaweed. Cook for 20 minutes.

5. After 20 minutes, remove the horseradish and seaweed from the wok.

6. Clean the mushrooms well and cut them into slices.

7. Cut the cod into cubes and put it in the wok. Also, add the mushrooms and bean sprouts.

8. Bring to a boil again and cook for 5 minutes, until the cod is cooked evenly.

9. Divide the soup into two bowls, add the red pepper slices and lemon slices, sprinkle with the chopped coriander and serve.

Dak During

Korean Recipes

Preapering	Servings	Cooking	Calories
20 Minutes	2 People	40 Minutes	250

Ingredients:

- 8.8 oz of chicken breast
- 1 potato
- 1 carrot
- ½ onion
- 1 tsp of seed oil
- 1 tsp of sesame seed oil
- 1 tbsp of soy sauce
- 1 minced garlic
- 1 tsp of gochujang
- 1 tsp of gochutgaru
- 2 tsp of honey
- The green part of 1 spring onion cut into thin slices
- Sesame seeds to taste

Nutritional Values:

Carb:	32 Gr.
Sugars:	15 Gr.
Proteins:	34 Gr.
Fats:	6 Gr.
Sodium:	575 Mg.

Steps for Cooking:

1. Peel the potato and carrot and cut them into cubes.

2. Peel the onion and slice it thinly.

3. Cut the chicken into pieces and sauté it in the wok with the hot seed oil.

4. Add a cup of hot water, garlic, gochutgaru, gochujang, honey, soy sauce, onion, potatoes and carrots.

5. Bring to a boil and cook over medium heat for about 30 minutes, the sauce must be reduced and all the ingredients must be well-cooked.

6. One minute before turning off the heat, add the sesame oil.

7. Now turn off the heat and sprinkle everything with sesame seeds and the spring onion.

8. Divide the Dak doritang between two plates and serve.

Dak Kalguksu

Korean Recipes

Preapering	Servings	Cooking	Calories
20 Minutes	2 People	55 Minutes	509

Ingredients:

- 4 oz noodles
- 5.2 oz of chicken thighs
- 1 tbsp of soy sauce
- 1 shallot
- 1 minced garlic clove
- 1 tbsp of sesame seed oil
- 1 tbsp of chili cream
- 2 cloves of garlic
- 1 zucchini

Nutritional Values:

Carb:	53 Gr.
Sugars:	23 Gr.
Proteins:	27 Gr.
Fats:	11 Gr.
Sodium:	1492 Mg.

Steps for Cooking:

1. Trim all skin, fat and sinew off the chicken thighs.

2. Put them in the wok and fill them with water. Bring to a boil over high heat, then reduce heat and simmer for 45 minutes.

3. After 45 minutes, remove the chicken legs from the cooking liquid and remove the meat from the legs by placing the meat in two bowls.

4. Season the chicken meat with the sesame oil, and the soy sauce and add the chili cream, mixing thoroughly to mix well.

5. Bring the chicken broth to a boil. Add the finely chopped garlic and shallot and add the tagliolini.

6. Cook for 10 minutes, then switch off. Divide the noodles and broth between the two bowls with the meat and serve.

Dakgalbi: Korean Marinated Chicken

Korean Recipes

Preapering	Servings	Cooking	Calories
20 Minutes	2 People	20 Minutes	402

Ingredients:

- 8.8 oz of chicken breast
- 1 onion
- 1 yellow pepper
- 1 potato
- 1 tsp of curry
- 1 tsp chili paste
- 1 tbsp of rice vinegar
- 2 tbsp of soy sauce
- 1 tsp of brown sugar
- 2 tsp of sesame seeds
- 1 tsp of fresh ginger
- Seed oil to taste

Nutritional Values:

Carb:	63 Gr.
Sugars:	16 Gr.
Proteins:	28 Gr.
Fats:	4 Gr.
Sodium:	1471 Mg.

Steps for Cooking:

1. Prepare the marinade by combining the soy sauce, rice vinegar, curry powder, chili paste, brown sugar, grated ginger and sesame seeds in a bowl.

2. Cut the chicken breast into equal pieces, put it in the bowl with the marinade and mix well.

3. Cover the bowl, put it in the fridge and marinate for 2 hours.

4. Peel the potato, wash it and cut it into cubes.

5. Wash the pepper and cut it into slices, peel the onion and cut it into slices.

6. Pour a little seed oil into the wok, let it heat up, then add the vegetables, salt lightly and cook over high heat for about ten minutes.

7. Add the chicken with all the marinade and cook, stirring constantly for another 10 minutes.

8. After cooking, divide the dakgalbi between two plates and serve.

Daikon with Perilla Seed Powder

Korean Recipes

Preapering	Servings	Cooking	Calories
20 Minutes	2 People	20 Minutes	180

Ingredients:

- 14 oz of daikon
- 1 minced garlic clove
- 1/2 teaspoon of salt
- 1 tablespoon of perilla seed powder
- ½ spring onion
- 2 tbsp of perilla or sesame seed oil
- ½ glass of water

Nutritional Values:

Carb:	16 Gr.
Sugars:	9 Gr.
Proteins:	2 Gr.
Fats:	3 Gr.
Sodium:	500 Mg.

Steps for Cooking:

1. Peel the daikon and cut it into sticks.

2. Wash and slice the onion.

3. Place the daikon and minced garlic in a bowl.

4. Add perilla oil, perilla seed powder, salt and water and mix well.

5. Heat the wok over medium heat, and then pour in the daikon and the contents of the bowl.

6. Cover the wok with the lid and cook for 10 minutes.

7. Add the spring onion, mix and cook for another 10 minutes over low heat with the lid on.

8. After cooking, divide the daikon and the cooking liquid between two plates and serve.

Dobu-Jorim

Korean Recipes

Preapering	Servings	Cooking	Calories
20 Minutes	2 People	10 Minutes	357

Ingredients:

- 7 oz of extra firm tofu
- 1 tsp of minced ginger
- 1 spring onion
- 1 minced garlic clove
- 1 tbsp of mirin
- 2 tbsp soy sauce
- 2 tsp of sesame seed oil
- 1 tsp brown sugar
- 1 tsp of gochutgaru
- Sesame seed oil to taste

Steps for Cooking:

1. Not too thin slices of tofu should be cut.

2. Slice the onion after washing it.

3. Ginger, spring onions, garlic, mirin, soy sauce, sesame oil, sugar, and gochugaru should all be combined in a bowl.

4. In the wok, heat the vegetable oil until it is hot. Brown the tofu on all sides after adding it.

5. Cook the tofu for 5 minutes after adding the hot sauce.

6. After the tofu has finished cooking, divide it into two dishes. Serve with a last drizzle of the wok's remaining sauce.

Nutritional Values:

Carb:	12 Gr.
Sugars:	4 Gr.
Proteins:	34 Gr.
Fats:	7 Gr.
Sodium:	574 Mg.

Chicken Strips, with Ginger, Hoisin Sauce & Soy Sauce

Korean Recipes

Preapering	Servings	Cooking	Calories
20 Minutes	2 People	25 Minutes	317

Ingredients:

- 8.8 oz of chicken breast
- 8.8 oz of mushrooms
- 8.8 oz of spinach
- 2 tbsp of soy sauce
- 1 clove of garlic
- 7 oz of basmati rice
- 1 tsp of freshly grated ginger
- 2 tbsp of hoisin sauce
- Olive oil to taste
- 1 tbsp of brown sugar
- Salt and pepper to taste

Nutritional Values:

Carb:	8 Gr.
Sugars:	4 Gr.
Proteins:	44 Gr.
Fats:	8 Gr.
Sodium:	634 Mg.

Steps for Cooking:

1. Peel the garlic and then grate it finely. Cut the chicken breast into strips.

2. Place the chicken in a bowl and add the soy sauce, ginger, half the minced garlic, 2 tbsp olive oil and the brown sugar.

3. Stir and leave to rest for the chicken to flavor well.

4. Meanwhile, in a medium saucepan, combine the rice and twice the amount of water as the rice. Add a little salt and bring to a boil over high heat, then cover the pot with the lid and reduce the heat to low.

5. Continue until cooked, it will take about 7 minutes. Shell the rice grains with a fork and keep the pot covered with the lid.

6. Clean the mushrooms, remove the stem and cut them into four parts. Wash the spinach well.

7. Heat 2 tbsp of oil in a wok and add mushrooms and spinach. Stir and cook for 5 minutes.

8. Add the chicken with the marinade and continue cooking over medium heat for 5 minutes.

9. Add the Hoisin sauce, a pinch of salt and pepper, and continue cooking for another 4 minutes over medium-low heat.

10. Once the chicken is cooked, switch off and divide the rice into two plates.

11. Add the chicken, mushrooms and spinach, sprinkle everything with the cooking juices and serve.

Korean Curry Rice

Korean Recipes

Preapering	Servings	Cooking	Calories
20 Minutes	2 People	25 Minutes	484

Ingredients:

- ½ onion
- ½ tsp of minced ginger
- 1 potato
- 1 carrot
- 2 mushrooms
- 3.5 oz of beef tenderloin
- 1 tbsp of curry powder
- 2 cups of water
- 1 cup of steamed rice
- Seed oil to taste
- Salt and pepper to taste

Nutritional Values:

Carb:	51 Gr.
Sugars:	11 Gr.
Proteins:	12 Gr.
Fats:	10 Gr.
Sodium:	800 Mg.

Steps for Cooking:

1. Peel the onion and cut it into wedges.

2. Peel the potato and carrot, wash them and then cut them into cubes of the same size.

3. Cut the beef into cubes. Heat a little seed oil in the wok and brown the beef for 2 minutes.

4. After 2 minutes, remove the beef and add the onion, potato and carrot.

5. Cook for 10 minutes, then add the ginger and cook for 1 minute.

6. Now pour in the water and bring it to a boil. Add the curry powder and stir until dissolved.

7. Lower the heat and simmer until the sauce thickens.

8. At this point, add the beef again, season with salt and pepper and cook for a couple of minutes.

9. Divide the steamed rice between two plates. Add the beef, vegetables and curry sauce and serve.

Jeyuk Bokkeum: Pan-Fried Pork with Spicy Sauce

Korean Recipes

Preapering	Servings	Cooking	Calories
25 Minutes	2 People	10 Minutes	331

Ingredients:

- 10.5 oz of pork shoulder
- ½ spring onion
- ½ onion
- 1 tbsp of soy sauce
- 1 tbsp of gochujang sauce
- 1 tsp of brown sugar
- 1 tsp of chili powder
- 2 tsp of rice wine or mirin
- 2 tsp of sesame oil
- 1 minced garlic clove
- 1 tsp of minced ginger
- ½ tsp of black pepper
- 1 tbsp of chopped apple
- Seed oil to taste

Nutritional Values:

Carb:	16 Gr.
Sugars:	12 Gr.
Proteins:	21 Gr.
Fats:	21 Gr.
Sodium:	785 Mg.

Steps for Cooking:

1. Wash and chop the onion and spring onion.

2. Cut the pork into thin strips.

3. Mix the soy sauce, rice wine, sesame oil, minced garlic, minced ginger, sugar, gochujang, gochutgaru and black pepper in a bowl.

4. Add the pork, mix well and marinate for 1 hour and 30 minutes.

5. Heat the vegetable oil in the wok over medium heat.

6. Add the meat, onion, spring onion, and marinade and cook for 8 minutes, stirring frequently.

7. Once cooked, divide the pork and the cooking liquid into two plates and serve.

Miyeok-Guk

Korean Recipes

Preapering	Servings	Cooking	Calories
20 Minutes	2 People	25 Minutes	351

Ingredients:

- 3.5 oz of beef pulp
- 2 tbsp of soy sauce
- 1 tsp of minced garlic
- 1 tbsp of dried and chopped seaweed
- 1 tbsp of sesame oil
- 4 glasses of water
- Salt and pepper to taste

Nutritional Values:

Carb:	3 Gr.
Sugars:	1 Gr.
Proteins:	24 Gr.
Fats:	6 Gr.
Sodium:	787 Mg.

Steps for Cooking:

1. Place the shredded beef tenderloin in a bowl and marinate with the minced garlic and 1 tbsp soy sauce.

2. Put the soaked seaweed in a bowl and keep it for 20 minutes. After 20 minutes, drain and set aside.

3. Put the sesame oil to heat in the wok. When the oil is hot, add the beef and sauté it for 3 minutes.

4. Add the seaweed and sauté for a few seconds. Then add the water and bring it to a boil.

5. As soon as it starts to boil, turn the heat down and add the other tbsp of soy sauce, salt, and pepper. Cook for 20 minutes, then switch off.

6. Divide the beef and broth between two bowls and serve.

Ojingeo Bokkeum: Squid in Spicy Sauce

Korean Recipes

Preapering	Servings	Cooking	Calories
25 Minutes	2 People	12 Minutes	380

Ingredients:

- 24.6 oz of squid
- 1 onion
- 1 carrot
- 1 spring onion
- 2 tbsp of soy sauce
- 1 tsp of chili powder
- 1 tsp of sugar
- 1 minced garlic clove
- 1 tbsp of gochujang chili paste
- 1 tbsp of mixed sesame seeds
- Sesame seed oil to taste

Nutritional Values:

Carb:	16 Gr.
Sugars:	1 Gr.
Proteins:	26 Gr.
Fats:	12 Gr.
Sodium:	800 Mg.

Steps for Cooking:

1. Wash the squid. Remove the innards, the beak, the skin and the shell. Cut the squid into strips and set aside.

2. Now prepare the sauce: mix the soy sauce, chili powder, chili paste, sugar and minced garlic.

3. Put the squid in the sauce and mix well.

4. Wash and slice the carrots diagonally and then into thin slices, cut the spring onion into small slices and slice the onion.

5. Heat some seed oil in the wok and let it heat up over medium heat.

6. Add the vegetables and sauté them for 3 minutes.

7. Add the squid and sauce and cook for another 5 minutes, stirring often.

8. Once cooked, add the sesame seeds and a little sesame oil and mix well.

9. Divide the calamari and sauce between two plates and serve.

Saeng Sun Jun

Korean Recipes

Preapering	Servings	Cooking	Calories
20 Minutes	2 People	10 Minutes	340

Ingredients:

- 2 cod fillets, 7 oz each
- 3 tbsp of flour
- 2 eggs
- Salt and black pepper to taste
- Seed oil to taste

Nutritional Values:

Carb:	15 Gr.
Sugars:	4 Gr.
Proteins:	34 Gr.
Fats:	7 Gr.
Sodium:	499 Mg.

Steps for Cooking:

1. Put the eggs in a bowl and beat them together with the salt and pepper.

2. Put the flour on a plate.

3. Cut the cod into two parts and dip it first in the eggs and then in the flour.

4. Heat the seed oil in the wok and as soon as it is hot, dip the cod fillets, one at a time.

5. Cook them on both sides until they are golden brown.

6. After cooking, remove the fish from the wok with the help of a slotted spoon to drain the excess oil.

7. Divide the fish into two plates and serve accompanied by hot sauce and soy sauce.

Sigumchi Namul

Korean Recipes

Preapering	Servings	Cooking	Calories
15 Minutes	2 People	10 Minutes	88

Ingredients:

- 14 oz of spinach
- 2 tbsp of soy sauce
- 1 tbsp of sesame seed oil
- 1 tbsp of toasted sesame seeds
- 1 tsp of salt
- 1 minced garlic clove
- 2 tsp of brown sugar

Nutritional Values:

Carb:	12 Gr.
Sugars:	11 Gr.
Proteins:	4 Gr.
Fats:	4 Gr.
Sodium:	375 Mg.

Steps for Cooking:

1. Wash the spinach and then blanch it in boiling water for 30 seconds.

2. Remove the spinach, drain and rinse in cold water.

3. Gently squeeze the spinach to remove excess water.

4. Heat a little seed oil in the wok and then pour the spinach.

5. Add soy sauce, salt, sugar and garlic and sauté for 3 minutes, stirring constantly.

6. After 3 minutes, switch off and sprinkle with sesame seeds.

7. Divide the spinach between two bowls, add the remaining sauce in the wok and serve.

Sogogi Mu Guk: Beef & Daikon Soup

Korean Recipes

Preapering	Servings	Cooking	Calories
20 Minutes	2 People	20 Minutes	365

Ingredients:

- 14 oz of beef pulp
- 7 oz of daikon
- 1 minced garlic clove
- ½ spring onion
- 1 tbsp of soy sauce
- 1 tbsp of sesame oil
- Salt and pepper to taste
- 2 cups of beef broth

Nutritional Values:

Carb:	10 Gr.
Sugars:	2 Gr.
Proteins:	36 Gr.
Fats:	10 Gr.
Sodium:	960 Mg.

Steps for Cooking:

1. Wash the daikon and cut it into cubes.

2. Separate the green part of the spring onion from the white one, wash and slice the green part and keep the white part.

3. Remove all the fat from the meat and then cut it into cubes.

4. Heat the wok over low heat, pour the sesame oil and fry the garlic and the meat for 2 minutes, being careful not to burn the garlic and the oil.

5. After 2 minutes, season with salt and pepper and add the broth.

6. Bring to a boil and cook for 10 minutes, then add the daikon, lower the heat, mix well and then pour in the soy sauce.

7. Cook until the daikon pieces are soft and translucent.

8. Finally, add the green part of the spring onion and switch it off.

9. Divide the meat and broth between two plates and serve.

Spinach Sujebi

Korean Recipes

Preapering	Servings	Cooking	Calories
40 Minutes	2 People	20 Minutes	378

Ingredients:

- 4 cups of water
- 1.7 oz of spinach
- 1 potato
- 1 zucchini
- 2.8 oz of shiitake mushrooms
- 2.8 oz of durum wheat flour
- Perilla seed powder to taste
- 2 tbsp of Soy Sauce

Nutritional Values:

Carb:	36 Gr.
Sugars:	12 Gr.
Proteins:	15 Gr.
Fats:	6 Gr.
Sodium:	952 Mg.

Steps for Cooking:

1. Put the spinach to cook with a tbsp of water in the wok, then drain it, put it in the blender and puree it.

2. Mix the spinach with the flour, adding a little water if necessary. Leave to rest in the fridge wrapped in transparent film for 30 min. The dough should be a little wet and sticky.

3. After 30 minutes, make the sujebi by pulling the dough and squeezing it, keeping the dough in the other hand.

4. Meanwhile, peel the potato and cut it into cubes, wash the zucchini and cut it into cubes, clean the mushrooms well and cut them into small pieces.

5. Put the mushrooms, a little seed oil, the zucchini and the mushrooms in the wok and sauté for 3 minutes.

6. Add the water and bring it to a boil. Add some salt and pepper and mix well.

7. Now add the sujebi and soy sauce and cook for another 10 minutes.

8. Mix the perilla seed powder with water in a small bowl and then add it to the broth. Cook for another 2 minutes and switch off.

9. Divide the spinach sujebi into two bowls, add the cooking liquid and serve.

Tteokbokki

Korean Recipes

Preapering	Servings	Cooking	Calories
20 Minutes	2 People	15 Minutes	438

Ingredients:

- 8.8 oz of rice dumplings
- 1 small carrot
- 1.7 oz of mushrooms
- 3.5 oz of beef
- 1 clove of garlic
- ½ small onion
- 1 small red pepper
- 1 small green pepper
- 2 tbsp of soy sauce
- 1 tsp of sesame oil
- 1 tsp of brown sugar
- 1 tsp of toasted sesame seeds
- Seed oil to taste

Nutritional Values:

Carb:	55 Gr.
Sugars:	15 Gr.
Proteins:	6 Gr.
Fats:	5 Gr.
Sodium:	300 Mg.

Steps for Cooking:

1. Cut the beef into strips and leave to marinate for 15 minutes in a bowl with the sugar, minced garlic clove, sesame oil and 1 tbsp soy sauce.

2. Wash the peppers, cut them first in half and then into strips.

3. Peel and wash the carrot and then cut it into sticks.

4. Remove the stem from the mushrooms, clean them well and then cut them into 4 parts. Peel and slice the onion.

5. Heat a little seed oil in the wok and sauté the onion slices for 1 minute.

6. Add the beef to the marinade, stir and cook for another minute.

7. Now add the mushrooms, the rice dumplings, the peppers and the carrot.

8. Add the other tbsp of soy sauce, stir and cook for 4 minutes.

9. Once cooked, divide the tteokbokki into two plates, sprinkle with sesame seeds and serve.

Tteokbokki with Soy Sauce

Korean Recipes

Preapering	Servings	Cooking	Calories
20 Minutes	2 People	20 Minutes	371

Ingredients:

- 3.5 oz of cylindrical shaped tteokbokki
- 1 tsp of rice malt syrup
- 2 tbsp of soy sauce
- 1 tbsp of mirin
- 1 tsp of seed oil
- 1 tbsp of sesame seed oil
- 1 tsp spring onion finely chopped, green part only
- Sesame seeds to taste

Steps for Cooking:

1. Prepare the sauce by mixing the soy sauce, syrup, mirin and sesame oil in a bowl.

2. Boil water in a saucepan and cook the tteokbokki following the package directions.

3. Heat the seed oil in the wok and put the drained tteokbokki. Sauté for a couple of minutes and then add the sauce.

4. Caramelize the sauce and tteokbokki well and then switch off.

5. Divide the tteokbokki between two serving plates and serve.

Nutritional Values:

Carb:	58 Gr.
Sugars:	15 Gr.
Proteins:	5 Gr.
Fats:	4 Gr.
Sodium:	400 Mg.

Vegan Bibimbap

Korean Recipes

Preapering	Servings	Cooking	Calories
20 Minutes	2 People	20 Minutes	400

Ingredients:

- 1 cup of basmati rice
- Sesame seed oil to taste
- 1 tbsp of soy sauce
- 1 carrot
- 7 oz of spinach
- 3.5 oz of broccoli florets
- 3 shitake mushrooms
- 1 tbsp ready-made fermented kimchi
- Toasted sesame seeds to taste

Nutritional Values:

Carb:	60 Gr.
Sugars:	20 Gr.
Proteins:	15 Gr.
Fats:	6 Gr.
Sodium:	910 Mg.

Steps for Cooking:

1. Rice should be steam-taped. When the rice is done, place it in a bowl and reserve it.

2. The carrots should be peeled and sliced into sticks.

3. Spinach should be cleaned, dried, and chopped roughly.

4. The broccoli blooms should be washed before being chopped into little pieces.

5. Sliced shitake mushrooms that have been cleaned.

6. The broccoli blooms are added to the hot pan and sautéed for 5 minutes.

7. Cook the spinach, mushrooms, and carrot for an additional 10 minutes.

8. Add the soy sauce and the chopped kimchi, combine well, and simmer for a few minutes.

9. Now turn out the lights, divide the vegan bibimbap between two dishes, top each with some steaming rice, and serve.

Chicken with Cashews

Thai Recipes

Preapering	Servings	Cooking	Calories
20 Minutes	2 People	15 Minutes	445

Ingredients:

- 10.5 oz of chicken breast
- 1.7 oz of cashews
- 2 tbsp of soy sauce
- 2 tsp of fish sauce
- ½ onion
- 1 tbsp of soybean oil
- 1 tbsp of rice flour
- Freshly grated ginger to taste
- Salt to taste
- 1 cup of cooked basmati rice
- 2 tbsp of water

Nutritional Values:

Carb:	20 Gr.
Sugars:	3 Gr.
Proteins:	46 Gr.
Fats:	19 Gr.
Sodium:	638 Mg.

Steps for Cooking:

1. Cut the chicken into cubes and put them in a bowl. Add the salt and rice flour and mix well.

2. Peel the onion and cut it into slices.

3. Put the cashews in the wok and toast them for a couple of minutes. Remove them from the wok and set them aside.

4. Now heat the oil in the wok and add the onion and ginger. Cook for 1 minute and then add the chicken.

5. Cook for 5 minutes. Season with salt and then add the soy sauce, water and cashews.

6. Cook for another 8 minutes or until the chicken is creamy.

7. Divide the cashew chicken between two plates, add the basmati rice and serve.

Coconut Fried Chicken

Thai Recipes

Preapering	Servings	Cooking	Calories
20 Minutes	2 People	15 Minutes	332

Ingredients:

- 7 oz of chicken breast
- 2 egg whites
- 5.2 oz of cornstarch
- Seed oil to taste
- ½ cup of coconut milk
- 2 tbsp of vinegar
- 2 tbsp of brown sugar
- 2 tbsp of coconut flour
- Salt and pepper to taste

Nutritional Values:

Carb:	26 Gr.
Sugars:	4 Gr.
Proteins:	33 Gr.
Fats:	6 Gr.
Sodium:	632 Mg.

Steps for Cooking:

1. Cut the chicken breast into cubes and season with salt and pepper.

2. Put the egg whites in a bowl and beat them with a fork. Place the chicken nuggets in the bowl and mix well.

3. Put the cornstarch in another bowl and stir until the chicken is completely covered.

4. Fill the wok with oil and heat it to high temperature.

5. Dip the chicken nuggets and cook them until they are well browned on the outside.

6. Remove the chicken nuggets with a slotted spoon and set aside.

7. Drain the oil and put the broth, coconut milk, vinegar, brown sugar and coconut flour in the wok. Mix well and then add the chicken.

8. Cook for 5 minutes, until the sauce, has completely thickened and switch off.

9. Divide the chicken and sauce between two plates and serve.

Coconut Lime Chicken

Thai Recipes

Preapering	Servings	Cooking	Calories
20 Minutes	2 People	15 Minutes	446

Ingredients:

- 7 oz of chicken breast
- ½ glass of coconut milk
- 2 tbsp coconut flour
- 1 tbsp flour
- ½ lime
- 1 bay leaf
- Salt and pepper to taste
- Peanut oil to taste

Nutritional Values:

Carb:	21 Gr.
Sugars:	0 Gr.
Proteins:	31 Gr.
Fats:	7 Gr.
Sodium:	243 Mg.

Steps for Cooking:

1. Cut the chicken breast into cubes and put it in a bowl.

2. Add the coconut flour, a little grated lime zest, the bay leaf and the flour. Mix everything well.

3. Heat the oil in the wok and then add the chicken. Brown well on all sides and then add the coconut milk, salt and pepper and mix.

4. Cook for 5 minutes, until the sauce, has thickened.

5. Once cooked, switch off, divide the chicken and the sauce into two bowls and serve.

Curried Pork

Thai Recipes

Preapering	Servings	Cooking	Calories
20 Minutes	2 People	25 Minutes	361

Ingredients:

- 7 oz of pork shoulder
- 1 minced garlic clove
- 1 tbsp of curry paste
- 1 tsp of cumin
- Fresh ginger minced to taste
- 4 tbsp of beef broth
- 1 glass of coconut milk
- 1 tbsp of fish sauce
- 1 tsp of brown sugar
- ½ lime
- 2 tsp of peanut butter

Nutritional Values:

Carb:	11 Gr.
Sugars:	5 Gr.
Proteins:	36 Gr.
Fats:	18 Gr.
Sodium:	412 Mg.

Steps for Cooking:

1. Cut the meat into cubes and put it in the bowl. Add the minced garlic, ginger, curry paste, cumin, half the coconut milk, the fish sauce, lime juice and sugar. Cover and leave to rest.

2. Put the remaining coconut milk, the broth, and the spoonful of curry pastes into the wok, add the peanut butter and cook for a few minutes.

3. Now add the fish sauce and a pinch of salt and cook until you get a creamy sauce.

4. Place the pork in the sauce and cook for 15 minutes, stirring frequently.

5. Once cooked, divide the pork and sauce into two bowls and serve.

Gai Pad Khing

Thai Recipes

Preapering	Servings	Cooking	Calories
20 Minutes	2 People	15 Minutes	491

Ingredients:

- 10.5 oz of chicken breast
- 2 tbsp of chopped fresh ginger
- 2 small onions
- 1.7 oz of carrots
- 3.5 oz of yellow peppers
- 1 Thai pepper
- 1 minced garlic clove
- 1 ½ tbsp of oyster sauce
- 1 tbsp of fish
- 1 tbsp of brown sugar
- Seed oil to taste

Nutritional Values:

Carb:	12 Gr.
Sugars:	2 Gr.
Proteins:	31 Gr.
Fats:	10 Gr.
Sodium:	376 Mg.

Steps for Cooking:

1. Wash the chicken breast and then cut it into cubes.

2. Wash the onions, and cut the white part into slices and the green part into rounds.

3. Peel the carrots, wash them and cut them into sticks.

4. Wash the peppers and cut them into strips.

5. In a bowl mix the oyster sauce, add the soy sauce, sugar and two teaspoons of fish sauce.

6. Heat the seed oil in the wok with the ginger, garlic and sliced Thai chili pepper.

7. Cook for 5 minutes, then add the chicken and spring onions and sauté for another 5 minutes.

8. Add a pinch of salt and 1 tbsp of vegetable oil, mix well and then add the peppers and carrots.

9. Cook for another 4 minutes then pour the sauce you prepared earlier.

10. Stir and add the fish sauce for flavor. Cook for 2 minutes and then switch off.

11. Divide the gai pad king between two plates and serve.

Gai Pad Prik Gaeng

Thai Recipes

Preapering	Servings	Cooking	Calories
20 Minutes	2 People	15 Minutes	477

Ingredients:

- 10.5 oz of chicken breast
- 7 oz of thai beans
- 1 ½ tbsp of red curry
- 2 lime leaves
- ½ tsp of palm sugar
- Fish sauce to taste
- 1 minced garlic clove
- 1 tbsp of peanut oil

Nutritional Values:

Carb:	24 Gr.
Sugars:	6 Gr.
Proteins:	42 Gr.
Fats:	9 Gr.
Sodium:	376 Mg.

Steps for Cooking:

1. Wash the green beans under running water. Drain them, remove the tips and cut them into pieces of equal size.

2. Wash the chicken breast and cut it into strips.

3. Heat the oil in the wok and then add the green beans. Saute for 1 minute, remove them from the wok and set aside.

4. Add more seed oil and cook the garlic for 2 minutes. Then add the chicken and brown it on all sides. Remove the chicken and keep it aside.

5. Add 1 tbsp of peanut oil and the curry paste, lime leaves and sugar to the stock, sauté for a few seconds to release the aromas, then put the chicken back.

6. Mix well and then add the fish sauce a little at a time. Check the flavor of the chicken each time before adding more fish sauce.

7. Continue cooking for another 5 minutes and then add the green beans.

8. Cook for another 3 minutes and then switch off.

9. Divide the Gai Pad Prik Gaeng into two plates and serve.

Khao Pad with Shrimp

Thai Recipes

Preapering	Servings	Cooking	Calories
20 Minutes	2 People	15 Minutes	421

Ingredients:

- 10.5 oz of shrimp tails
- 5.6 oz of basmati rice
- 1 carrot
- 5.2 oz of peas
- 2 eggs
- 2 spring onions
- 4 tbsp of seed oil
- 2 tbsp of soy sauce
- 1 lime
- 1 tsp of brown sugar
- 1 tbsp of chopped parsley
- 1 minced garlic clove

Nutritional Values:

Carb:	42 Gr.
Sugars:	6 Gr.
Proteins:	24 Gr.
Fats:	12 Gr.
Sodium:	364 Mg.

Steps for Cooking:

1. Boil a pot of lightly salted water and cook the rice until cooked through, usually about 14 minutes.

2. Once cooked, quickly cool the rice under cold water and drain very well.

3. Cut the spring onions into slices, using both the white and green parts and keep them aside, then peel the carrot and cut it into small cubes, chop the garlic clove and keep everything aside.

4. Wash the shrimp tails and remove the intestinal filament if it is still present. Rinse the shrimp again.

5. Heat 2 tbsp of seed oil in the wok and as soon as it is hot, sauté the carrot and spring onions for 2 minutes.

6. Add the eggs to the pan and cook them, stirring frequently, so that they set and break into strips.

7. When the eggs are set, add 1 tbsp of vegetable oil, the minced garlic clove, the prawn tails and the peas and cook for a few minutes, stirring often until the prawn tails are cooked too.

8. In a small bowl, mix 2 tbsp soy sauce and 1 tbsp brown sugar, then stir well to dissolve the sugar.

9. Now add the shrimp tails, mix well and sauté for a couple of minutes together with the soy sauce.

10. Turn off and sprinkle with chopped parsley. Divide the sautéed rice with the vegetables into two bowls and serve.

Pad Thai

Thai Recipes

Preapering	Servings	Cooking	Calories
20 Minutes	2 People	20 Minutes	609

Ingredients:

- 5.2 oz of rice noodles
- 2.6 oz of bean sprouts
- 2 tbsp of seed oil
- 1 tbsp of chopped coriander
- 1 tbsp of fish sauce
- 1 tbsp of soy sauce
- 7 oz of black tiger prawns
- 1.4 oz of peanuts
- 1 tbsp of tamarind juice
- 1 clove of garlic
- 1 tsp chopped chives

Nutritional Values:

Carb:	71 Gr.
Sugars:	4 Gr.
Proteins:	21 Gr.
Fats:	16 Gr.
Sodium:	379 Mg.

Steps for Cooking:

1. Start by covering the rice noodles with warm water and let them soak until it's time to cook.

2. Heat the wok and the seed oil for 2 minutes and then add the peanuts. Toast them for a few minutes, stirring frequently to prevent them from burning.

3. Remove the peanuts from the wok, place them on a plate and set aside.

4. Now add the minced garlic and fry them for 2 minutes.

5. Now pour the drained rice noodles and let them infuse, stirring constantly.

6. Now add the soy sauce, tamarind juice and fish sauce and mix again.

7. Pour in two tablespoons of water, the chives, the bean sprouts and the coriander, raise the heat and mix well.

8. Move the rice noodles to a corner of the wok and make room for the prawns, which you have previously shelled and washed well under running water.

9. Sear them for two minutes on each side, then mix the prawns with the rest of the ingredients.

10. Finally, add the toasted peanuts, mix and when everything is well incorporated, switch off, divide the Pad Thai into two plates and serve.

Pad Thai with Chicken

Thai Recipes

Preapering	Servings	Cooking	Calories
25 Minutes	2 People	20 Minutes	721

Ingredients:

- 7 oz of rice noodles
- 5.2 oz of chicken breast
- 3.5 oz of tofu
- 1 egg
- 1 tbsp of tamarind sauce
- 1 tbsp of palm sugar
- 1 tbsp of fish sauce
- 1 tbsp of soy sauce
- Peanut oil to taste
- ½ shallot
- 1 minced garlic clove
- 3.5 oz of bean sprouts
- 1 spring onion
- Chopped pepper to taste
- ½ carrot
- Roasted peanuts to taste

Nutritional Values:

Carb:	54 Gr.
Sugars:	15 Gr.
Proteins:	0 Gr.
Fats:	12 Gr.
Sodium:	390 Mg.

Steps for Cooking:

1. Put the noodles to rehydrate in cold water, leaving them to soak for about 15 minutes. Peel the shallot and chop it finely.

2. Start preparing the sauce by frying the shallots, garlic and finely chopped chili pepper in a wok with a little peanut oil; add the palm sugar, tamarind paste, soy sauce and fish sauce, stir and cook until the sugar has completely dissolved.

3. Let the sauce thicken, then remove it from the wok and put it in a bowl.

4. Cut the tofu and chicken into cubes.

5. Add more seed oil to the wok and when hot, add the chicken and tofu.

6. Sauté for 6 minutes, stirring frequently. Now add the shelled egg and mix continuously.

7. Add the drained noodles, and the previously prepared sauce and mix everything for a few minutes.

8. Cut the green part of the spring onion into rings and add it to the wok together with the bean sprouts and the carrot cut into julienne strips.

9. Sauté over high heat until all ingredients are well blended.

10. Finally add the toasted peanuts, mix and switch off. Divide the Pad Thai between two bowls and serve.

Panang Chicken & Peanut Curry

Thai Recipes

Preapering	Servings	Cooking	Calories
20 Minutes	2 People	30 Minutes	579

Ingredients:

- 8.8 oz of boneless chicken thighs
- ½ cup of coconut milk
- 2 tbsp of cream of coconut
- 1 tbsp Panang curry
- 2 lime leaves
- 2 tsp of fish sauce
- 3 tbsp of roasted peanuts
- 1.7 oz of pineapple slices
- 2 tsp of lime juice
- 2 tsp of peanut oil
- 1 tsp of brown sugar
- ½ chopped onion
- 1 tsp Hot Chili Sauce
- 7 Thai basil leaves

Nutritional Values:

Carb:	19 Gr.
Sugars:	12 Gr.
Proteins:	48 Gr.
Fats:	19 Gr.
Sodium:	0 Mg.

Steps for Cooking:

1. Heat the seed oil in the wok and sauté the onion with the curry over medium heat for about 2 minutes.

2. Add the coconut milk and bring to a boil.

3. Put the chicken cut into small pieces and the lime leaves, lower the heat and cook for 15 minutes.

4. Remove the chicken with the help of a slotted spoon and set aside.

5. Let the sauce thicken for 5 minutes.

6. Add the coconut cream, fish sauce, lime juice and sugar and cook for another 5 minutes.

7. Now put the chicken back in the wok and cook for 2 minutes.

8. Now add the basil, the diced pineapple and the toasted peanuts.

9. Mix well, finally add the chili sauce and switch off.

10. Divide the chicken into two bowls, add the remaining sauce to the wok and serve with steamed Thai rice.

Red Curry with Pork

Thai Recipes

Preapering	Servings	Cooking	Calories
20 Minutes	2 People	30 Minutes	470

Ingredients:

- 8.8 oz of pork shoulder
- 1 glass of coconut milk
- 4 basil leaves
- 2 lime leaves
- 2 Thai red chilies
- 2 cloves of minced garlic
- 2 tsp of shrimp paste
- 2 tsp of minced ginger
- 1 tbsp of lemon grass
- 2 tsp of palm sugar
- Fish sauce to taste

Nutritional Values:

Carb:	5 Gr.
Sugars:	2 Gr.
Proteins:	31 Gr.
Fats:	15 Gr.
Sodium:	342 Mg.

Steps for Cooking:

1. Start by preparing the curry paste: soak the peppers in warm water for 20 minutes.

2. After 20 minutes, take the peppers and chop them.

3. Put the chilies, ginger, lemon grass, garlic and a tsp of salt in the mixer.

4. Add the shrimp paste and mix well.

5. Wash the meat, pat it dry with a paper towel and then cut it into cubes.

6. Put the coconut milk in the wok, heat it up and then add the curry paste. Mix and bring to a boil.

7. Add the meat, fish sauce and sugar and mix well. Cook for 5 minutes over low heat, stirring occasionally.

8. Add the lime leaves and basil leaves and more fish sauce if needed.

9. Cook until the sauce has reduced.

10. Once cooked, divide the meat and curry into two bowls and serve.

Shrimp Green Curry

Thai Recipes

Preapering	Servings	Cooking	Calories
25 Minutes	2 People	20 Minutes	409

Ingredients:

- 5.2 oz of shrimp
- ½ glass of coconut milk
- ½ glass of vegetable broth
- 1 tbsp of soy sauce
- 2 tsp of green curry paste
- 1.7 oz of green beans
- 1 zucchini
- 1 minced garlic clove
- 1 spring onion
- Chopped ginger to taste
- 2 tbsp of sunflower oil
- Salt and pepper to taste

Nutritional Values:

Carb:	16 Gr.
Sugars:	8 Gr.
Proteins:	36 Gr.
Fats:	12 Gr.
Sodium:	416 Mg.

Steps for Cooking:

1. Shell the shrimp, remove the intestinal filament and then wash them.

2. Wash the green beans, peel them and then divide them into 3 parts.

3. Trim the zucchini, wash it and then cut it into cubes.

4. Wash the onion and cut it into slices.

5. Heat the oil in the wok, then add the grated ginger, garlic, spring onion and curry paste.

6. Leave to flavor for a few minutes, then add the coconut milk, soy sauce, broth and zucchini cubes.

7. After 10 minutes, add the green beans, salt and pepper and leave to infuse for a few seconds.

8. Cook for another 10 minutes, then add the shrimp and cook for another 5 minutes.

9. Once cooked, divide the prawns, green beans and curry sauce and serve.

Spicy Pork Salad

Thai Recipes

Preapering	Servings	Cooking	Calories
20 Minutes	2 People	35 Minutes	385

Ingredients:

- 10.5 oz of chopped pork loin
- 1 tbsp of glutinous rice
- 2.6 oz of shallots
- 1 lime
- 1 tbsp of chopped fresh coriander
- 1 Thai pepper
- 1 tbsp of fish sauce

Nutritional Values:

Carb:	8 Gr.
Sugars:	3 Gr.
Proteins:	32 Gr.
Fats:	20 Gr.
Sodium:	332 Mg.

Steps for Cooking:

1. Put the rice in the mixer, activate it and chop for a few seconds.

2. Now pour the rice into the wok and toast it until it reaches a golden colour.

3. Remove the rice from the wok and set it aside.

4. Peel the shallots and cut them first in half and then into julienne strips.

5. Put the minced pork loin in the wok add 3 tbsp of water and the fish sauce.

6. Add the chopped Thai pepper and turn on the flame.

7. Let the meat cook, putting the lid on the wok and stirring occasionally, for about 20 minutes.

8. After 20 minutes, remove the lid and cook for another 10 minutes.

9. When the meat is cooked, turn off the flame and add the shallots. Stir to heat up the shallots.

10. Transfer the meat and shallots to a salad bowl and let it cool completely.

11. When the meat has cooled, add the coriander and mix.

Thai Chicken Curry with Green Beans

Thai Recipes

Preapering	Servings	Cooking	Calories
20 Minutes	2 People	20 Minutes	462

Ingredients:

- 8.8 oz of chicken breast
- ½ onion
- 1 minced garlic clove
- 1 minced Thai pepper
- 1 tbsp of chopped coriander
- 1 tsp of cumin seeds
- ½ tsp of turmeric powder
- 5.2 oz of green beans
- 1 tsp of tomato paste
- ½ cup of coconut milk
- 2 tsp of curry paste

Nutritional Values:

Carb:	13 Gr.
Sugars:	6 Gr.
Proteins:	33 Gr.
Fats:	12 Gr.
Sodium:	310 Mg.

Steps for Cooking:

1. Peel the onion and cut it into slices.

2. Trim the green beans, wash them and cut them in half.

3. Cut the chicken breast into cubes.

4. Put the oil in the wok and add the cumin seeds first, then the garlic and the sliced onions and let them soften slightly.

5. Add the turmeric, chili and tomato paste, mix and add the diced chicken breast and green beans.

6. Add a pinch of salt, mix well and cook for a couple of minutes.

7. Dissolve the curry paste in the coconut milk and add them to the wok.

8. Place the lid on the wok and cook for 10 minutes, until the meat is cooked through and the sauce thick.

9. Turn off and sprinkle with the chopped coriander.

10. Divide the chicken, green beans and curry sauce between two bowls and serve.

Thai Curry with Potatoes & Chicken

Thai Recipes

Preapering	Servings	Cooking	Calories
20 Minutes	2 People	45 Minutes	526

Ingredients:

- 2 chicken drumsticks
- 2 tbsp of red curry paste
- 3.5 oz of potatoes
- 1 glass of coconut milk
- ½ onion
- 4 tbsp of roasted peanuts
- 1 tbsp of tamarind pulp
- ½ lemon
- 1 tsp of brown sugar
- ½ tsp of cardamom seeds
- 1 bay leaf
- ½ cinnamon stick
- 1 tbsp of coconut oil
- Fish sauce to taste

Nutritional Values:

Carb:	48 Gr.
Sugars:	14 Gr.
Proteins:	38 Gr.
Fats:	16 Gr.
Sodium:	385 Mg.

Steps for Cooking:

1. Remove the skin from the chicken drumsticks, wash them and put them in the wok.

2. Add the cardamom seeds, cinnamon, bay leaf and a pinch of salt.

3. Pour in half of the coconut milk and add enough water to completely cover the chicken.

4. Bring to a boil and cook over medium heat for 25 minutes or until the meat is tender.

5. Meanwhile, peel the onion and potatoes and cut them into small pieces. In another wok, heat the coconut oil.

6. Add the curry paste and mix. Cook over low heat for about a minute, mixing well. Pour in the remaining coconut milk and mix. Bring to a boil and cook for another 5 minutes.

7. Add the potatoes and onions and add a ladleful of the chicken cooking liquid.

8. Cook for 2 minutes then add the lemon juice, tamarind paste and sugar.

9. Mix well, add the peanuts and fish sauce and cook for 15 minutes, or until the potatoes are soft.

10. After 25 minutes, take the chicken and put it in the wok with the potatoes. Mix well, let it cook for a few minutes and then turn it off.

11. Put the potatoes and the chicken in two bowls, cover them with the curry and serve.

Thai Red Shrimp Curry

Thai Recipes

Preapering	Servings	Cooking	Calories
25 Minutes	2 People	25 Minutes	355

Ingredients:

- 10.5 oz of shrimp
- 1 cup of coconut milk
- 1 tbsp of minced ginger
- 2 Thai red chilies
- 2 lime leaves
- 2 cloves of minced garlic
- ½ lime
- 1 tbsp of chopped coriander
- 2 sprigs of lemongrass
- Fish sauce to taste
- Sesame seeds to taste

Steps for Cooking:

1. Shell the shrimp and wash them thoroughly under running water.

2. Put the chilies, garlic, lemongrass leaves and ginger in a hand-blender container. Blend until you get a homogeneous paste.

3. Put the coconut milk in the wok and bring it to a boil. Now add the curry paste.

4. Mix well and when the pasta is incorporated add the shrimp and a little fish sauce.

5. Cook for 5 minutes, then add the lime leaves.

6. Divide the prawn curry between two bowls and add the sliced lime, chopped coriander and sesame seeds and serve.

Nutritional Values:

Carb:	15 Gr.
Sugars:	4 Gr.
Proteins:	24 Gr.
Fats:	6 Gr.
Sodium:	650 Mg.

Thai-Style Hot & Spicy Tofu

Thai Recipes

Preapering	Servings	Cooking	Calories
20 Minutes	2 People	15 Minutes	213

Ingredients:

- 5.2 oz of tofu
- 2 tbsp of chopped walnuts
- 2 tsp of chopped lemongrass
- 2 tsp of chopped coriander
- 2 tbsp of Thai fish sauce
- 2 tsp of peanut oil
- 1 tbsp of seed oil
- 8.8 oz of bok choi
- 8.8 oz of broccoli
- 1 lime
- 2 tsp of sweet chili sauce

Nutritional Values:

Carb:	7 Gr.
Sugars:	2 Gr.
Proteins:	12 Gr.
Fats:	7 Gr.
Sodium:	200 Mg.

Steps for Cooking:

1. Mix the diced tofu, walnuts, lemon grass, coriander, fish sauce and peanut oil in a bowl.

2. Cover and leave to marinate at room temperature for 2 hours.

3. Remove the bock choi, wash the leaves and cut them into small pieces.

4. Remove the stem from the broccoli and then wash the flowers, then cut the broccoli into small pieces.

5. Heat the vegetable oil in the wok and then add the broccoli and bok choi.

6. Cook until the vegetables are tender.

7. Remove the vegetables and keep them aside. Add the tofu and marinade and cook for 5 minutes.

8. Add the chili sauce, and lime juice and sauté for another 2 minutes.

9. Put the vegetables, mix and cook for 1 minute.

10. After cooking, put the tofu, the vegetables and the cooking juices on two plates and serve.

Tofu & Sweet Potato Curry

Thai Recipes

Preapering	Servings	Cooking	Calories
20 Minutes	2 People	25 Minutes	391

Ingredients:

- ½ tbsp of peanut oil
- 7 oz of tofu
- 6.3 oz of coconut milk
- ½ cup of vegetable broth
- 1 tbsp of Thai red curry paste
- 7 oz of sweet potatoes
- 2 tsp of fish sauce
- 1 tsp of coconut sugar
- 1 tbsp of lime juice
- 4 basil leaves
- ½ tsp of paprika

Nutritional Values:

Carb:	20 Gr.
Sugars:	8 Gr.
Proteins:	16 Gr.
Fats:	10 Gr.
Sodium:	290 Mg.

Steps for Cooking:

1. Cut the tofu into cubes. Do the same with sweet potatoes.

2. Heat the peanut oil in the wok together with the paprika.

3. Add the tofu and sauté it, turning it on all sides until it is golden brown.

4. Remove the tofu from the wok and add the coconut milk and vegetable stock and bring to a boil.

5. Add the curry paste, stir and cook for 4 minutes.

6. Now pour in the sweet potatoes, stir and cook over medium heat for 10 minutes.

7. Incorporate the sugar, the fish sauce, the lime juice, and continue cooking for another 5 minutes.

8. Add the basil leaves cut into strips, put the tofu back in and cook for 1 minute.

9. Now turn off the stove, put the tofu and sweet potatoes on two plates, cover them with the curry sauce and serve.

Tom Kha Gai

Thai Recipes

Preapering	Servings	Cooking	Calories
20 Minutes	2 People	20 Minutes	450

Ingredients:

- 3.5 oz of chicken breast
- ½ stalk of lemongrass
- 1 lime
- 1 shallot
- ½ thay peppers chopped
- ½ tbsp of fish sauce
- ½ cup of coconut milk
- ½ cup of chicken broth
- 1 tbsp of lemon juice
- 1 tbsp of fresh coriander

Steps for Cooking:

1. Put the chicken broth in the wok to boil together with the lemongrass, the lime zest and the peeled and sliced shallot.

2. Cut the chicken into cubes and put it in the wok. Also add the coconut milk, fish sauce, Thai chili and lemon juice.

3. Bring to a boil again and continue cooking for another 3 minutes.

4. As soon as the chicken is cooked, turn off the heat and sprinkle with the chopped coriander.

5. Pour the Tom Khai Gai into two plates and serve.

Nutritional Values:

Carb:	12 Gr.
Sugars:	5 Gr.
Proteins:	31 Gr.
Fats:	15 Gr.
Sodium:	420 Mg.

Tom Yum Kung

Thai Recipes

Preapering	Servings	Cooking	Calories
30 Minutes	2 People	20 Minutes	330

Ingredients:

- 10.5 oz of whole shrimp
- 4 moss mushrooms
- 2 tbsp of bamboo shoots
- 2 cups of chicken broth
- ½ tbsp of tom yum mix
- ½ tsp of nam pla sauce
- 1 tsp of brown sugar
- 1 sprig of coriander
- 1 hot red pepper

Nutritional Values:

Carb:	13 Gr.
Sugars:	3 Gr.
Proteins:	32 Gr.
Fats:	6 Gr.
Sodium:	670 Mg.

Steps for Cooking:

1. Slice the bamboo stalks after placing them on a chopping board.

2. Divide the moss mushrooms in half.

3. Slice the pepper into tiny pieces after removing the seeds.

4. Chop the coriander after washing it.

5. Wash the prawns, remove the intestinal filament, then shell them with care to leave the head and tails on.

6. Bring a small amount of water to a boil in the wok. Boil the moss mushrooms and bamboo shoots for one minute in the wok.

7. Place the bamboo shoots and mushrooms on a platter after draining them.

8. Bamboo stalks and musk mushrooms are now added to the wok along with the chicken stock when it has reached a boil.

9. Mix after adding the tom yum mix. Dip the prawns into the broth after bringing it back to a boil.

10. After one minute of cooking, stir in the nam pla, sugar, and chili pepper.

11. Switch off the stovetop at this point, then divide the tom yum kung between two dishes and serve.